# How to Understand Sewing Symbols: Your Essential Visual Dictionary for Every Stitch and Seam

PUBLISHED BY Peter Whitmore

© **Copyright 2025 - All rights reserved.**

All introductions, analyses, and commentaries contained within this book may not be reproduced, duplicated, or transmitted without direct written permission from the author or the publisher. Under no circumstances will any blame or legal responsibility be held against the publisher or author for any damages, reparation, or monetary loss due to the information contained within this book, either directly or indirectly.

**Legal Notice:**

This book is only for personal use. You cannot amend, distribute, sell, use, quote, or paraphrase any part of the introductions, analyses, or commentaries within this book, without the consent of the author or publisher.

**Disclaimer Notice:**

Please note the information contained within this document is for educational and entertainment purposes only. All efforts have been executed to present accurate, up-to-date, reliable, complete information. No warranties of any kind are declared or implied. Readers acknowledge that the author is not engaged in the rendering of legal, financial, medical, or professional advice. The content within this book has been derived from various sources. Please consult a licensed professional before attempting any techniques outlined in this book.

By reading this document, the reader agrees that under no circumstances is the author responsible for any losses, direct or indirect, that are incurred as a result of the use of the information contained within this document, including, but not limited to, errors, omissions, or inaccuracies.

# Table of contents

Introduction .......................................................................... 4

Chapter 1: The Historical Evolution of Sewing Notation Systems ............................................................ 10

Chapter 2: Decoding Pattern Markings and Construction Lines .................................................... 23

Chapter 3: Fabric Behavior and Treatment Icons ... 34

Chapter 4: Hardware and Notion Placement Diagrams ........................................................................ 44

Chapter 5: Seam Construction and Finishing Techniques ...................................................................... 55

Chapter 6: Three-Dimensional Shaping Symbols .... 66

Chapter 7: Professional Tailoring and Couture Symbols ............................................................................ 76

Chapter 8: Industrial and Mass Production Symbols ............................................................................................ 87

Chapter 9: Digital Pattern and Smart Textile Symbols ............................................................................................ 97

Chapter 10: Specialty Techniques and Cultural Symbols ......................................................................... 108

Conclusion ..................................................................... 118

# Introduction

Imagine opening a sewing pattern for the very first time. The lines, dashes, triangles, circles, arrows, and other curious marks can appear like an indecipherable code, one that only the most experienced seamstresses and tailors could possibly understand. To the uninitiated, these markings might feel intimidating, as though you've stumbled upon a secret language passed down through generations of makers. Yet, once you begin to learn their meanings, these symbols reveal themselves not as barriers but as gateways to creativity, precision, and connection with a global community of artisans. Sewing symbols are, in many ways, the grammar of fabric—the visual shorthand that allows makers from Tokyo to Toronto, from Milan to Mumbai, to communicate design, structure, and technique without uttering a single word.

This "visual grammar" has evolved over centuries of practical necessity. Every craft requires a system of representation that is both efficient and universally accessible. Just as mathematicians rely on equations or musicians on notation, sewists have cultivated a language of marks that transcends borders and spoken tongues. Unlike written language, which must be translated into countless versions, sewing symbols often remain consistent in meaning across cultures. A simple dotted line can signify stitching placement, a triangle might indicate where to match seams, and a small circle could guide you in aligning darts. Once mastered, these tiny cues unlock the ability to bring a flat piece of fabric into a structured, three-dimensional form.

What makes sewing symbols so fascinating is that they sit at the intersection of art and engineering. A sewing pattern, after all, is both blueprint and poem. On one hand, it provides precise, technical instructions that ensure a garment holds together and fits the human form. On the other hand, it allows the maker to express style, mood, and identity through choice of fabric, color, and finishing. Symbols serve as the scaffolding that supports this balance. They free the maker from verbose explanations, compressing entire paragraphs of instruction into a single mark that fits neatly onto a pattern piece. In doing so, they maintain the flow of creativity while guaranteeing accuracy and repeatability.

This universality is what makes sewing symbols so powerful. A dressmaker in Paris can open a Japanese pattern magazine and, without speaking the language, follow the instructions with confidence. A quilter in Brazil can swap templates with a friend in Canada and still achieve the same precise results. Even when regional variations exist—and they do—the foundation of sewing notation is so broadly shared that adaptation comes naturally. In this way, sewing symbols create a bridge across cultures, a silent pact among makers that says: "I understand you, and I know what you mean." They become a form of collaboration that is not bound by nationality, dialect, or even era.

Of course, this visual language did not emerge fully formed. Its history reflects the broader evolution of sewing itself. In earlier centuries, before industrial printing, tailors and seamstresses often relied on guild secrets, oral traditions, and individualized systems of marking. These were not intended for widespread communication but rather to protect trade knowledge within tight-knit communities. The rise of mass-produced clothing and printed patterns in the 19th century began to shift this insular practice into a standardized system. Suddenly, symbols needed to be understood by a far wider audience—home sewists, factory workers, and students in sewing schools. What began as guarded shorthand grew into a globally recognized vocabulary.

Today, the necessity of sewing symbols has only deepened. As digital platforms and international commerce bring patterns to a worldwide audience, symbols serve as the glue that makes cross-border exchange possible. You can purchase a PDF pattern online from a designer halfway across the world, print it at home, and confidently decode its meaning without needing to translate every word. This efficiency has fueled a renaissance in sewing communities, enabling independent pattern designers to reach international markets and hobbyists to access resources that once felt geographically out of reach. Symbols thus act as both practical tools and cultural ambassadors.

Yet for all their importance, sewing symbols remain an area that often confuses beginners and frustrates even intermediate makers. Unlike written instructions, which can be read at leisure, symbols require a kind of visual literacy. You must learn to distinguish between subtle variations: a solid line versus a dashed one, a small notch versus a large one, or an arrow pointing in one direction rather than another. Misinterpreting a single symbol can alter the outcome of an entire project. A dart placed incorrectly can distort the fit of a garment; a seam allowance ignored can shrink the dimensions of a quilt. Understanding symbols, therefore, is not merely about memorization but about cultivating a fluent ability to read patterns with clarity and confidence.

This book exists to serve as your guide into that literacy. Think of it as your visual dictionary—an atlas to the world of sewing notation. Just as you might consult a dictionary to clarify an unfamiliar word, here you will find clear explanations and illustrations of every common symbol used across sewing disciplines. Whether you are piecing together a tailored jacket, a patchwork quilt, or a simple tote bag, this resource will demystify the marks on your pattern and empower you to sew with both skill and independence. More than just a glossary, however, this book will situate each symbol in context. You will not only learn *what* it means but also *why* it matters, how it functions in relation to the fabric, and how to apply it correctly in your own projects.

The idea of sewing as a "universal language" extends beyond practicality. At its heart, it speaks to the collaborative spirit of making. Sewing has always been more than the act of stitching fabric together; it is a means of storytelling, identity, and cultural continuity. Patterns passed down within families often bear markings familiar only to those who inherit them, creating threads of connection between generations. Symbols recorded in books or shared in classrooms spread knowledge across time, linking us with the hands that came before and the hands that will come after. To learn these symbols, then, is to participate in a legacy—one that is as much about community as it is about craft.

Moreover, decoding this visual grammar can instill a profound sense of confidence. For many beginners, sewing can feel overwhelming: measurements to take, fabrics to choose, machines to master. Symbols, once understood, provide anchors of certainty within that complexity. They reassure you that you are on the right track, that the garment will come together as intended, and that you are not navigating the process alone. Each symbol carries with it the accumulated knowledge of countless makers, distilled into a simple sign. By reading them fluently, you step into that tradition and allow it to guide your hands.

As you embark on this journey, consider the humility and ingenuity embodied in such a system. In an age dominated by complex technologies, sewing symbols remind us that human beings are capable of creating elegant solutions through simplicity. A triangle, a line, a circle—these modest shapes contain the wisdom to transform raw fabric into clothing, to shape textiles into objects of beauty and function. They reveal how much can be accomplished with very little, provided there is clarity of thought and collective agreement. This principle mirrors the very essence of sewing itself: the ability to craft something enduring and meaningful out of basic materials.

In the chapters that follow, you will encounter not just a catalog of marks but a philosophy of making. You will come to appreciate how these symbols interlock like pieces of a puzzle, how they speak to one another on the page, and how they guide your hands in harmony with the fabric. You will see how minor variations can influence construction, and how mastering this visual grammar unlocks freedom for experimentation. Once you are fluent, patterns cease to feel like rigid instructions and instead become flexible tools—frameworks upon which you can build your own ideas and innovations.

Ultimately, understanding sewing symbols means learning to see beyond the marks themselves. They are not arbitrary decorations, nor are they meant to intimidate. They are invitations—signposts pointing the way toward mastery and self-expression. By embracing them, you step into a shared world where creativity and clarity coexist, where makers across cultures and centuries join together in a silent but unmistakable dialogue. This is the universal language of sewing: concise, powerful, and unifying.

With it, you are never truly alone at your craft table, for you are part of a community that stretches far beyond your own walls.

Let us begin, then, with the basics of this language. Open your patterns with fresh eyes, ready to decode their grammar and uncover their wisdom. Once you learn to read them, you will find that every stitch, seam, and fold speaks the same truth: that creativity has always been, and will always remain, a language without borders.

# Chapter 1: The Historical Evolution of Sewing Notation Systems

*"Before the first standardized sewing symbol appeared in 1947, seamstresses relied on over 200 different regional marking systems across Europe alone, leading to countless misinterpretations and ruined garments."*

## 1.1 From Guild Marks to Global Standards

To understand why sewing symbols feel so indispensable today, one must step back into a time when such visual grammar barely existed, or when it was guarded like a code of power. The evolution from scattered regional markings to an internationally recognized system is not just a story about tailoring; it is a narrative about secrecy, commerce, cultural identity, and eventually, the pressures of industrialization and war. Sewing symbols, after all, were never born in isolation. They grew out of human necessity: the need to protect professional skills, the need to share patterns across borders, and the need to mass-produce clothing on a scale history had never seen before.

## The Hidden Language of the Guilds

In medieval Europe, tailoring was not simply a trade—it was a profession tightly regulated by guilds. These guilds functioned as both training institutions and protective associations, ensuring that only qualified members could profit from specialized knowledge. Among the many secrets guarded were the ways in which patterns were recorded and transmitted. Fabric was expensive, time was precious, and a well-fitted garment was a sign of both skill and social status. Because of this, guild members often developed their own "cipher" systems—small sets of marks, notches, or coded drawings—that only fellow initiates could interpret.

Imagine a master tailor passing down his knowledge to an apprentice. Instead of writing lengthy instructions, he would scratch cryptic signs onto parchment or directly onto cloth. A circle with a slash might indicate a pleat, while a cross could signal where two pieces must align. These symbols were never standardized. They were idiosyncratic, bound to the tradition of a single workshop or town. To outsiders, they looked like meaningless scratches, but within the guild, they represented a language of precision. Such ciphers ensured that the craft remained protected. Even if a written pattern fell into the hands of an untrained seamstress, it could not easily be copied without the insider's key.

This secrecy had two major consequences. On one hand, it preserved the economic value of the tailor's craft, shielding it from those who might undercut prices by imitating designs. On the other, it stifled broader communication. A symbol that meant "cut here" in one city might mean "stitch here" in another, leading to misunderstandings whenever patterns circulated beyond their local context. In many cases, garments made outside of their intended region would not fit properly, both literally and figuratively, into another culture's system of making.

The guild cipher systems mirrored the guarded nature of other medieval professions. Just as stonemasons left coded marks on cathedral stones or alchemists recorded formulas in riddles, tailors used symbols to keep their art both practical and mysterious. It was not until centuries later that necessity pushed these marks into the public sphere.

## The Great Exhibition and the Dream of Universality

The Industrial Revolution radically altered the conditions of sewing. Textile production accelerated, garments could be produced at lower costs, and printed publications circulated widely. By the mid-19th century, an increasing number of people outside professional guilds—especially women sewing at home—were engaging with patterns. Commercial pattern companies began to emerge, each creating their own sets of markings to guide users. But without a shared standard, confusion abounded.

The 1851 Great Exhibition in London, a monumental showcase of industrial and cultural achievements, became an unexpected stage for this problem. Among the displays of steam engines, glass architecture, and manufactured goods, sewing patterns appeared as artifacts of progress. International exhibitors presented their methods, and in doing so, revealed the striking lack of agreement. What was a simple notch to one exhibitor meant something entirely different to another. An arrow that directed fabric orientation in France might be misread as a pleat marker in Germany.

The Exhibition, while meant to highlight innovation, inadvertently exposed the impossibility of universal comprehension. Committees attempted to discuss the idea of a common system of sewing notation, but cultural differences and pride in national practices quickly derailed the conversation. Each country had built its methods on long-standing traditions, and no nation wished to abandon its approach in favor of another's. Moreover, sewing was not seen as an urgent industrial concern compared to engines, telegraphs, or metallurgy. The idea of a universal symbol system was shelved, dismissed as impractical.

For the next century, this lack of agreement persisted. Regional publishers and companies developed their own marks, leading to a patchwork of systems. This suited local markets but became problematic as international trade grew. By the early 20th century, with more women purchasing paper patterns from abroad, misunderstandings multiplied. One misplaced dart or misread seam allowance could ruin an entire garment. In many ways, the seeds of frustration experienced by countless home sewists in this era can be traced back to the failure of 1851.

## War, Mass Production, and the Birth of Standards

It would take the devastation of World War II to force a change. During the war years, clothing production had to be efficient, uniform, and understandable across vast populations of workers, many of whom had little previous experience with sewing. Military uniforms, hospital garments, and civilian clothing under rationing schemes required rapid and standardized methods. Factories could not afford delays caused by pattern misinterpretations.

Governments and industry leaders realized that fragmented systems of symbols were no longer tolerable. If hundreds of women working in a British textile factory misread a pleat mark, entire batches of uniforms could be wasted at a time when material shortages were severe. The solution was clear: symbols needed to be standardized, not for artistic pride but for survival.

By the mid-1940s, committees in Europe and North America began convening to establish uniform sets of sewing marks. This was not an academic exercise but an urgent matter of wartime logistics. The first widely recognized standardized sewing symbols emerged around 1947, just as nations rebuilt in the aftermath of conflict. For the first time, pattern companies agreed on basic visual cues: how to indicate cutting lines, seam allowances, darts, pleats, and notches.

This shift represented more than technical efficiency; it symbolized the democratization of sewing knowledge. What had once been the secret code of guilds now belonged to everyone. Home sewists could purchase patterns with confidence, regardless of the publisher, and follow them with far less risk of error. Factories could train workers more quickly, relying on consistent notation. Schools could teach students using textbooks that mirrored what they would find in commercial patterns.

It is striking to consider that the very same forces that devastated much of the world also gave birth to the common language of sewing we recognize today. War demanded clarity, and clarity gave way to standardization. What medieval guilds had hoarded, what the Great Exhibition had failed to achieve, was finally realized out of sheer necessity.

## A Legacy of Shared Understanding

The establishment of standardized symbols did not erase all regional variations, but it created a core vocabulary that remains recognizable. It also set the stage for later innovations, including the digital systems of the 20th and 21st centuries. Today, when you see a dashed line, a double arrow, or a dart symbol, you are reading the outcome of centuries of trial, secrecy, failure, and global crisis. Behind that simple mark lies the memory of guild apprentices bent over dimly lit workrooms, of exhibitors proudly defending national traditions, and of wartime factory workers stitching uniforms with urgency.

The journey from guild marks to global standards is, at heart, a reminder of how human beings respond to necessity. When pride and secrecy ruled, symbols remained fragmented. When curiosity and competition dominated, attempts at universality faltered. But when survival itself required clarity, consensus finally emerged. Sewing notation, like language itself, reflects the conditions of its time: the need to protect, the urge to share, and the demand to survive.

## 1.2 The Digital Revolution in Symbol Communication

The standardization of sewing symbols after the Second World War provided an essential common ground for communication, but the arrival of digital technologies in the late twentieth century propelled the evolution of these marks into a new era. Until the 1980s, most pattern makers continued to rely on manual drafting. Designers sketched their lines directly onto paper, annotated them by hand, and copied them using tracing or printing methods. Symbols were functional but often inconsistent in execution, depending heavily on the skill of the drafter and the accuracy of reproduction. A seam line might appear clear on an original sheet but blur or distort after several photocopies. This variability was acceptable in small-scale use but increasingly problematic as the fashion industry demanded speed, accuracy, and global consistency.

Computer-aided design, or CAD, offered a solution. First applied to engineering and architecture, CAD systems began to influence the fashion and textile industries in the 1980s. With the introduction of digital drafting, sewing symbols could finally be rendered with absolute precision. A notch, arrow, or dart drawn on a computer screen appeared crisp and identical every time it was reproduced, whether in New York or Seoul. This shift was transformative. No longer were symbols dependent on a drafter's hand or the quality of reproduction; they became standardized digital elements, easily copied, resized, or adjusted without loss of clarity.

Beyond precision, CAD enabled an entirely new scale of pattern manipulation. Designers could grade patterns—adjust them for different sizes—with far greater ease, and the accompanying symbols scaled with perfect proportion. A dart symbol on a size 6 bodice remained visually identical to that on a size 16, preserving its meaning without distortion. The result was both efficiency for industry professionals and a more reliable product for home sewists purchasing printed patterns. For the first time, sewing symbols were not only consistent in meaning but also uniform in appearance across the globe.

As the digital revolution progressed, the question became how to embed these symbols into broader technological systems. The rise of the internet in the 1990s and early 2000s created unprecedented opportunities for pattern sharing. Designers could now send patterns as digital files, bypassing the limitations of physical print. Yet for these exchanges to work, the symbols needed to be universally readable across computer systems. This led to a turning point in 2010, when sewing symbols were formally incorporated into Unicode, the global standard for text and symbol encoding.

The significance of this inclusion cannot be overstated. Unicode functions as a kind of universal alphabet for computers, ensuring that symbols appear consistently regardless of platform, software, or device. Before 2010, a pattern file created on one system might display incorrectly on another, leading to frustration or even unintentional errors in garment construction. With Unicode support, sewing symbols became part of the digital infrastructure of communication. A dart symbol embedded in a PDF file could be opened anywhere in the world, on any device, with full fidelity. This moment effectively globalized the language of sewing symbols, placing them on equal footing with letters, numerals, and mathematical operators.

The 2010 milestone also dovetailed with the rise of independent pattern designers selling PDFs online. A small business owner in Buenos Aires could now design a dress, encode the necessary symbols, and distribute the pattern to customers worldwide without worrying that a pleat mark would render incorrectly. This democratization of access fostered a new ecosystem of creativity, particularly for hobbyists and small-scale entrepreneurs. Sewing symbols, once confined to professional guilds and later industrial systems, now belonged to a truly global public with unprecedented ease of use.

The latest frontier of this digital revolution lies in augmented reality and QR-coded systems. While paper remains the most common medium for patterns, experiments with overlay technologies suggest a future where symbols are no longer static marks on a page but interactive guides in real time. Some developers have begun embedding QR codes into patterns, which, when scanned, link to symbol libraries or animated instructions. Instead of puzzling over a dart symbol, a sewist can scan the code and watch a demonstration video explaining how to fold and stitch it. This hybridization of static notation with digital augmentation reduces the learning curve and expands accessibility for beginners.

More ambitious still are augmented reality applications that project sewing symbols directly onto fabric. Using a tablet or specialized glasses, a maker can align fabric pieces while the device overlays cutting lines, seam allowances, or placement marks onto the material itself. This eliminates the possibility of misreading symbols on paper and bridges the gap between two-dimensional instructions and three-dimensional construction. Although still in its early stages, this technology represents the logical extension of the visual grammar of sewing: a language that began as scribbles in guild notebooks, became standardized through war, refined by CAD, and is now merging with the immersive possibilities of digital interactivity.

The digital revolution thus transformed sewing symbols from local shorthand into a globally reliable language. It enhanced precision, ensured universal readability, and opened the door to interactive teaching. Far from replacing the traditional craft, these developments expanded its possibilities, enabling more people to learn, share, and innovate than ever before.

## 1.3 Regional Variations That Still Persist

Despite the sweeping march toward standardization, sewing symbols have never become entirely uniform. Local traditions, cultural metaphors, and proprietary systems continue to shape how certain symbols are drawn or understood. This persistence of variation is not necessarily a flaw but rather a reminder that sewing, while practical, is also deeply tied to identity and heritage. Even in a world connected by Unicode and digital files, some symbols retain their distinctly regional flavors.

One of the most striking examples comes from Japan, where the tradition of *wasai*—the art of Japanese garment construction—employs symbols that draw upon seasonal and poetic imagery. Instead of relying solely on geometric arrows to indicate fabric grain direction, some *wasai* manuals employ metaphors rooted in nature. The vertical grain may be compared to bamboo growing upward, while diagonal alignment may be represented through symbols suggesting wind or flowing water. These metaphoric indicators not only serve a functional purpose but also reinforce the cultural philosophy of harmony between fabric, wearer, and environment. For a Japanese sewist, reading these symbols is as much about understanding rhythm and balance as it is about technical alignment. To outsiders, these markings may appear unusual or even obscure, but they reflect a worldview in which sewing is inseparable from natural cycles.

In Europe, particularly within haute couture houses, variation persists not from cultural metaphor but from deliberate exclusivity. Prestigious ateliers often maintain proprietary sets of symbols for hand-finishing techniques. These marks do not appear in mass-market patterns but are reserved for the internal use of master seamstresses working on custom garments. A unique symbol might denote a specific type of hand-applied hemstitch, another might indicate a finishing method known only within that house. The rationale for this secrecy is partly tradition and partly branding. Just as medieval guilds protected their knowledge through ciphers, modern couture houses protect their techniques through private notation. To work within such an atelier requires fluency in its internal system, reinforcing the exclusivity of the craft.

Beyond the structured worlds of *wasai* and haute couture, there are also textile traditions that use symbols entirely outside the Western lineage of sewing notation. Many Indigenous communities incorporate pictographic symbols into their textiles, symbols that are not merely functional but also carry cultural and spiritual significance. In certain Native American traditions, motifs woven or embroidered into garments serve both as technical markers for construction and as storytelling devices, conveying clan identity or ancestral narratives. Similarly, in

Andean weaving practices, symbols often guide the alignment of threads on a loom while simultaneously expressing cosmological beliefs. These markings cannot be reduced to simple equivalents of darts or notches; they exist at the intersection of craft, language, and spirituality.

What unites these regional variations is their refusal to fully conform to the standardized vocabulary established in the mid-20th century. While a dashed line or triangular notch may be universally recognizable, these other systems remind us that sewing is not only a technical act but also a cultural one. Symbols function not just as instructions but as carriers of meaning, identity, and heritage. For a Japanese seamstress interpreting a bamboo symbol, or an apprentice in a Parisian atelier decoding a proprietary mark, the act of sewing connects them to a lineage larger than the fabric itself.

The persistence of variation also underscores a paradox at the heart of sewing notation. On the one hand, global consistency makes patterns accessible and reduces errors, a vital advantage in industrial and hobbyist contexts alike. On the other, variation preserves the richness of local traditions and keeps alive the sense of uniqueness that standardized marks sometimes flatten. This tension is unlikely to resolve fully, nor should it. Just as spoken languages adapt to global communication while maintaining dialects, sewing symbols can serve as a universal grammar while allowing for local accents.

Taken together, the digital revolution and the endurance of regional variation reveal the complexity of sewing's visual language. It is at once global and local, standardized and idiosyncratic, practical and poetic. To understand sewing symbols fully is not only to learn what they mean in a textbook sense but also to appreciate the contexts in which they live. Some tell us where to cut, fold, or stitch; others remind us of bamboo swaying in the wind, a couture house's closely held secret, or an ancestral story woven into cloth. They are marks that carry both utility and memory, binding the act of sewing to the broader human story.

# Chapter 2: Decoding Pattern Markings and Construction Lines

*"A single misread grainline symbol costs the fashion industry an estimated $2.3 million annually in wasted luxury fabric."*

## 2.1 Essential Pattern Perimeter Symbols

When approaching a sewing pattern, the first symbols you are likely to encounter are those that mark the perimeter of each piece. These symbols are not decorative; they are the foundational cues that determine how fabric is cut, how it is oriented, and how one piece aligns with another during construction. A line that may seem no more than a dash with an arrowhead carries within it an instruction that, if ignored, can make the difference between a garment that drapes elegantly and one that twists awkwardly on the body. To the untrained eye, perimeter symbols may look like simple lines and arrows, but to the experienced sewist, they are the grammar of fit and form.

## Grainline Arrows and Their Variations

Perhaps the most recognizable and essential perimeter marking is the grainline arrow. This long arrow, usually stretching across a pattern piece, indicates how the piece should be aligned with the grain of the fabric. Fabric grain refers to the direction of the threads woven or knitted to form the cloth. Warp threads run lengthwise, parallel to the selvage edge, while weft threads run crosswise. The grainline symbol ensures that a garment's structural and aesthetic qualities remain intact by anchoring the pattern piece to this invisible architecture.

The standard grainline arrow is a simple, straight line with arrowheads at both ends. Its placement communicates that the pattern piece must be laid parallel to the fabric's lengthwise grain, usually aligning with the selvage. If this symbol is misread or ignored, disastrous results can follow. A bodice cut off-grain will twist after washing, trousers will sag at the knees, and tailored garments will refuse to hang smoothly. In industrial production, even a small misalignment repeated across hundreds of garments results in enormous financial losses, which is why grainline accuracy has been calculated to cost millions in wasted fabric annually in luxury fashion.

Beyond the standard grainline, there are multi-directional variations that provide greater nuance. Some arrows include branching or angled lines, signaling that the piece may be cut along either the lengthwise or crosswise grain. This flexibility is often found in casual garments or linings where drape is more forgiving. More advanced still are bias indicators, often represented by arrows drawn at a 45-degree angle across the pattern piece. Cutting on the bias—diagonally across the grain—produces a garment with unique drape, elasticity, and movement. Iconic bias-cut dresses of the 1930s owe their fluid silhouettes to this practice. The bias grainline symbol, though simple in appearance, thus communicates an entire philosophy of design. It tells the sewist that the fabric's natural stretch is not only tolerated but embraced as part of the garment's intended effect.

# Fold Line Variations

Another critical perimeter symbol is the fold line, which indicates that a pattern piece should be placed along the fabric's folded edge. This ensures that when the fabric is cut, the resulting piece is symmetrical, with no seam down the center. Common in bodices, skirts, and yokes, fold lines save time and fabric while preserving design integrity. The most straightforward fold line symbol is a heavy arrow or bracket that runs along the edge of the pattern piece, pointing toward the fold.

However, variations exist that demand closer attention. Some fold lines are marked with zigzag patterns, indicating a simple fold for symmetry. Others use double or even triple zigzags to suggest accordion folds, pleats, or layered folds within the same piece. A sewist who overlooks these distinctions risks flattening a three-dimensional design into a two-dimensional cut. For example, pleated skirts often rely on carefully marked fold lines that indicate not only where fabric is folded but also in which direction and how many times. Misreading these lines results in uneven pleats, disrupted symmetry, and garments that fail to capture the intended volume.

Complex pleat notations often combine fold lines with directional arrows that show whether fabric should be folded inward or outward. In certain haute couture and theatrical costumes, accordion pleat symbols indicate that fabric must be folded multiple times in alternating directions. These markings might look confusing at first glance, but once decoded, they reveal a method for transforming flat fabric into sculptural form. The artistry of pleats, tucks, and gathers begins with these modest yet powerful symbols.

## Seam Allowance Indicators

While grainlines and fold lines govern placement and symmetry, seam allowance indicators control the invisible margins where pieces join together. A seam allowance is the strip of fabric between the stitching line and the raw edge, and its width is crucial to both durability and fit. Too narrow a seam allowance risks fraying and weak seams, while too wide an allowance adds unnecessary bulk.

Symbols for seam allowances vary across metric, imperial, and industrial systems, making them particularly important for sewists working with patterns from different countries. In many commercial patterns in the United States, a standard seam allowance of five-eighths of an inch is built into the pattern, with the stitching line represented by a dashed line inside the cutting line. In European systems, particularly those influenced by German and Scandinavian drafting traditions, seam allowances are often excluded from the printed pattern and must be added manually. Symbols in these cases often include a double line at the perimeter or annotations in millimeters, such as "+10 mm," instructing the sewist to add the allowance when cutting.

Industrial systems, used in factories for mass production, frequently adopt narrower allowances, sometimes as little as one centimeter, to save fabric and streamline construction. In these contexts, seam allowance indicators may appear as fine parallel lines with precise measurements annotated directly on the pattern. The difference between a home pattern and an industrial one can thus be dramatic, and the symbols guiding seam allowances must be read carefully to avoid error.

Confusion often arises when sewists move between systems. A pattern designed for home sewing may expect the sewist to follow a generous allowance, while a factory-trained maker might instinctively trim too closely. In multilingual or international pattern books, seam allowance symbols act as silent translators, making clear whether the sewist should add, subtract, or trust the printed line. Without this guidance, even an experienced maker can find seams that fail to match, hems that fall unevenly, and garments that fit poorly.

## The Interplay of Perimeter Symbols

Grainlines, fold lines, and seam allowances may appear as discrete elements, but in practice they work together as a system. A grainline arrow establishes the orientation of the piece, the fold line dictates symmetry, and the seam allowance defines the invisible architecture of joining. When read in combination, these perimeter symbols create a framework for both design and durability. They are the navigational compass of pattern reading, guiding the sewist from raw fabric to finished garment.

For the beginner, these marks may feel intimidating, but with practice, they reveal their logic. A long arrow is not just a line but a promise that fabric will drape correctly. A zigzag fold line is not just a decoration but an instruction to create depth and volume. A seam allowance indicator is not just a number but a safeguard against fraying and distortion. Together, these perimeter symbols shape the garment before the first stitch is ever made.

In many ways, they also embody the paradox of sewing symbols as a whole: they are at once simple and profound. A straight line with arrows is easy to draw, yet it represents centuries of accumulated knowledge about fabric behavior. A zigzag mark may take seconds to sketch, yet it unlocks the complex geometry of pleating. A double line with a small number printed beside it may seem insignificant, yet it governs the strength of a seam and the comfort of the wearer. To learn these symbols is to acquire not only technical competence but also a sensitivity to the subtle interplay between design, fabric, and construction.

As we progress further into the language of sewing, it becomes clear that these essential perimeter symbols form the foundation upon which all other markings rest. Without them, the interior notations—darts, notches, placement marks—would float without context. With them, the sewist possesses a clear map, a reliable guide to transforming pattern paper into lived clothing.

## 2.2 Internal Pattern Navigation Markers

Once the perimeter of a pattern piece is established by grainlines, fold lines, and seam allowances, the eye of the sewist must move inward. The interior of a pattern sheet is often crowded with marks that look puzzling to the beginner but carry essential information about how the flat fabric will eventually shape the three-dimensional garment. These internal navigation markers guide everything from contouring the body to distributing fullness, aligning complex prints, and ensuring that seams meet where they should. To read them accurately is to learn the choreography of garment construction, for these symbols dictate how fabric must be shaped, eased, and joined.

Among the most important of these symbols are darts and their variations. A dart is a wedge-shaped fold of fabric sewn into the garment to provide shape, often contouring fabric around the bust, waist, or hips. On a pattern, darts are usually drawn as two angled lines that converge at a single point, sometimes accompanied by small dots or notches that indicate where stitching should begin and end. While a simple dart may seem straightforward, the symbols associated with dart manipulation reveal how dynamic they can be. Rotational transformation indicators, for instance, demonstrate how darts can be shifted around the body without altering the overall fit. A series of arrows drawn around a pivot point suggests that the fullness represented by a dart may be relocated—rotated from the side seam to the waistline, from the shoulder seam to the bust point, or even distributed across multiple smaller darts. This flexibility allows designers to control not only fit but also style, using the same underlying measurements to achieve dramatically different visual effects. To the sewist who understands these symbols, a dart is no longer a fixed element but a movable tool of design.

Equally important within the pattern interior are marks that control ease distribution. Ease refers to the intentional difference between the body's measurements and the garment's measurements, a small but vital allowance that enables movement, comfort, and drape. Ease marks are often represented by clusters of small notches or parallel slashes along a seam line, showing where fabric must be gathered or stretched to fit another piece. These marks are not arbitrary; they follow proportional systems that balance fullness evenly across a seam. In sleeve construction, for example, ease marks at the sleeve cap indicate where fabric should be gently distributed so the sleeve fits smoothly into the armhole without puckering. Without these marks, a sewist might distribute gathers unevenly, leading to distortion and discomfort. The mathematical underpinning of these symbols—whether dividing excess fabric into thirds or distributing it symmetrically around a central axis—remains invisible to the eye but is embedded in the marks themselves. They are the visual residue of geometric calculations made by the pattern drafter, simplified into cues that anyone can follow.

Pattern navigation also involves matching points, especially when dealing with complex fabrics such as stripes, plaids, or directional prints. These are often marked by small triangles, diamonds, or crosses placed along seam lines. While they may look like minor notations, their importance cannot be overstated. When a striped fabric must meet precisely at a side seam, or when the squares of a plaid must align across a pocket and bodice, these matching points ensure visual continuity. Ignoring them leads to jarring mismatches that disrupt the intended design. In mass production, such mistakes can devalue entire garment runs, while in bespoke tailoring, they mark the difference between amateur and master craftsmanship. Reading and respecting these alignment markers elevates the final garment from merely functional to aesthetically refined, honoring the designer's vision and the fabric's potential.

Taken together, darts, ease marks, and pattern matching points exemplify how internal navigation symbols transform the flat geometry of paper into the lived reality of clothing. They are the silent stage directions that guide fabric into curves, fullness, and harmony. To overlook them is to risk garments that pull, gape, or jar the eye. To master them is to wield the invisible power of shaping and alignment that separates ordinary sewing from the art of garment construction.

## 2.3 Size Grading and Adjustment Symbols

While internal navigation symbols govern how a garment is constructed, grading and adjustment symbols ensure that it can be adapted to different bodies. No two people are exactly alike, and the challenge of pattern making lies not only in shaping fabric but in scaling it across a spectrum of sizes and proportions. Grading systems emerged to address this challenge, and the symbols that accompany them provide a roadmap for both industrial production and personal customization.

One of the most recognizable features of modern patterns is the presence of nested grading lines. On a single sheet, multiple outlines of the same garment appear layered like concentric shapes, each corresponding to a different size. These lines are often distinguished by variations in dashes, dots, or colors, and each is labeled with an alphanumeric code such as "10," "12," "14," or "S," "M," "L." To the untrained eye, the result can look chaotic, but these nested lines are in fact a condensed atlas of the garment across body types. By tracing the correct line, the sewist selects the size that best matches their measurements. In professional contexts, nested grading symbols also provide manufacturers with efficient ways to cut multiple sizes from a single master pattern. Misreading these lines, however, can be costly. Following the wrong dash style or size code can result in cutting the wrong size altogether, wasting fabric and time.

Closely related to nested grading lines are adjustment zones for lengthening or shortening. These areas are often marked by parallel lines running horizontally across a pattern piece, accompanied by annotations such as "Lengthen or Shorten Here." These symbols identify safe zones where the garment's proportions can be altered without distorting its design. For instance, a dress bodice may need to be lengthened for a taller wearer, but adding length at the hem would throw off the placement of the waistline. Instead, the pattern provides a designated adjustment zone, ensuring that alterations maintain balance. The ratios indicated in these symbols are more than arbitrary. They reflect careful proportional systems developed by pattern drafters, ensuring that the relationship between garment sections—shoulder to bust, bust to waist, waist to hip—remains harmonious. Without these guides, adjustments risk producing garments that feel off-balance or awkwardly proportioned.

Another increasingly common set of symbols reflects the reality that many individuals do not fit neatly into a single size category. Blend size indicators help sewists transition smoothly between sizes within a single garment. On a nested pattern, a sewist might find that their bust corresponds to a size 12, their waist to a size 14, and their hips to a size 10. Blend size indicators, often represented by curved transition lines or annotated instructions, show where and how to merge these sizes without disrupting the garment's design. For example, a gentle curve connecting size 12 at the bust to size 14 at the waist ensures a natural fit, whereas a sharp or uneven adjustment would cause distortion. These blending marks embody the growing recognition that bodies are not standardized. They empower sewists to create garments that respect individual proportions rather than forcing conformity to rigid size categories.

The significance of grading and adjustment symbols extends beyond personal customization. In industrial contexts, they underpin the economics of fashion. Grading systems allow a single design to be sold in dozens of sizes, expanding markets and reducing the need for separate patterns for each measurement. Adjustment zones and blend indicators, meanwhile, reflect a more human-centered approach, acknowledging the diversity of real bodies. Together, these symbols bridge the gap between the universal and the individual, between mass production and personal fit.

For the sewist, learning to read grading and adjustment symbols unlocks the ability to adapt patterns confidently. No longer must they accept a pattern "as is." With an understanding of nested lines, adjustment zones, and blending guides, they can mold designs to their own body or to the bodies of those they sew for. This not only ensures comfort and style but also extends the life of patterns, which can be reused across multiple projects with different measurements. What at first glance appear as bewildering clusters of lines and annotations are, in fact, the keys to a garment's adaptability and longevity.

# Chapter 3: Fabric Behavior and Treatment Icons

*"Professional pattern makers use over 150 distinct symbols just to indicate fabric properties—more than twice the number of letters in most alphabets."*

## 3.1 Textile Structure and Composition Indicators

When a sewist unfolds a pattern, the sheet is not merely a map of shapes to be cut and assembled. It is also a coded document that communicates how the chosen fabric will behave and how it must be handled to achieve the intended result. Unlike perimeter or construction marks, which govern fit and assembly, fabric behavior symbols deal with the inherent qualities of the textile itself. They answer questions about weave, fiber content, stretch, and resilience, questions that determine not just whether a garment will come together, but whether it will perform as envisioned when worn. Without these indicators, a pattern risks becoming abstract geometry, divorced from the material reality of cloth.

One of the oldest and most fundamental categories of fabric behavior symbols concerns weave structure. A plain weave, the simplest interlacing of warp and weft threads, is often represented by a grid-like symbol on a pattern or in its accompanying documentation. This symbol communicates not just the physical structure but the expectations attached to it: stability, even surface texture, and a relatively firm drape. As one moves beyond plain weave, symbols grow more intricate. A twill, with its characteristic diagonal ribs, is indicated by diagonal lines across the grid, signaling greater flexibility, a smoother drape, and higher durability. Satin weave symbols replace diagonals with staggered gaps, showing where warp threads float over multiple weft threads to create sheen and fluidity. More elaborate still are jacquard indicators, often depicted as complex geometric motifs within the weave grid, suggesting patterns woven directly into the fabric. For the sewist, the ability to decode these symbols provides an instant understanding of how a garment will fall, stretch, and reflect light, even before touching the fabric itself. It is a form of tactile literacy transferred into visual shorthand.

Fiber content symbols form another crucial set of textile indicators. While weave dictates the physical structure, fiber content determines much of the fabric's performance: warmth, breathability, resilience, and care requirements. A pictograph of a cotton boll might represent cotton fibers, while a stylized sheep indicates wool, and a triangular leaf signals linen derived from flax. Synthetic fibers such as polyester, nylon, or acrylic often appear as chemical flask icons or abstract geometric shapes suggesting artificial origin. Beyond single-fiber indicators, modern patterns frequently include blend markers, specifying the percentage composition of different fibers. A garment symbol may be annotated with "65/35" alongside cotton and polyester icons, immediately telling the sewist that the fabric combines natural comfort with synthetic durability. These blend markers are not trivial. A misread fiber symbol could lead a sewist to choose a fabric that reacts poorly to pressing, shrinks unpredictably after washing, or fails to drape as required. The pictographs serve as both warnings and guides, ensuring that the maker's choice of fabric aligns with the designer's vision.

Stretch indicators represent one of the more recent developments in textile notation, reflecting the increasing use of knits, elastane blends, and performance fabrics. A typical stretch symbol consists of arrows placed along the edge of a fabric swatch drawing, showing the direction and degree of stretch. Double-headed arrows pointing horizontally across the symbol suggest two-way stretch, while arrows in both horizontal and vertical directions signify four-way stretch. Accompanying these directional arrows are often percentage indicators, such as "20% stretch" or "50% stretch," specifying how much the fabric can elongate relative to its original length. These numbers are not arbitrary; they are calculated through standardized tests where fabric is pulled under controlled force. For the sewist, they communicate critical information. A pattern designed for 50% stretch fabric will not fit properly if made with cloth that stretches only 10%. Misinterpreting such a symbol can result in garments that are either impossibly tight or slack and shapeless.

Closely tied to stretch symbols are recovery rate indicators. Stretch alone does not guarantee performance; the question is whether the fabric returns to its original shape after being stretched. Recovery is represented by curved arrows that loop back onto themselves, sometimes paired with numerical percentages. A fabric with 90% recovery will spring back almost fully after being stretched, maintaining shape and fit, while a fabric with 50% recovery will sag, bag, or grow during wear. These symbols are particularly important in activewear, swimwear, and lingerie, where both stretch and recovery determine comfort and longevity. Without them, a sewist might select a fabric that performs well in the short term but deteriorates quickly, leading to disappointment.

The interplay of weave, fiber, stretch, and recovery indicators paints a holistic picture of fabric behavior. Consider a pattern symbolized with a twill weave mark, a wool pictograph, a 20% stretch arrow, and an 85% recovery loop. From these symbols alone, an informed sewist can deduce that the designer intends the garment to be made of a wool twill with moderate elasticity, suitable for tailored trousers that move with the wearer but retain crisp lines. Contrast this with a pattern marked with satin weave, silk fiber, and no stretch arrows, which signals an elegant, fluid garment best suited for formal occasions. In both cases, the sewist does not need paragraphs of description; the symbols condense this knowledge into a compact visual grammar.

These textile indicators also reflect a deeper truth about the relationship between pattern and fabric. A paper pattern, however carefully drafted, is only half the story. The other half lies in the cloth, which brings its own properties and limitations to the equation. Symbols for weave, fiber, stretch, and recovery act as bridges between these two halves, ensuring that the abstract geometry of the pattern harmonizes with the physical character of the textile. Without them, the sewist risks treating all fabrics as interchangeable, a mistake that inevitably leads to garments that look or feel wrong.

It is worth noting that the development of these symbols was not merely an academic exercise but a response to practical problems. In earlier decades, many home sewists learned by costly trial and error, discovering only after construction that their chosen fabric stretched too little, wrinkled too easily, or shrank too much. By the mid-twentieth century, as fabric technology expanded to include synthetics and blends, the need for clear visual indicators became pressing. Fiber content and care labels addressed consumers, but pattern symbols addressed makers, guiding them to select fabric not just for aesthetics but for compatibility with construction.

In contemporary practice, textile structure and composition indicators have expanded alongside advances in fabric technology. Patterns for sportswear, for instance, often include symbols for moisture-wicking fibers, breathable mesh zones, or UV-protective textiles. Though not universally standardized, these icons extend the same principle: compressing complex information into quick, universally readable marks. As fabrics become more specialized, the role of symbols grows more vital, preventing confusion and ensuring that sewists can keep pace with innovation.

Learning to decode these textile indicators is thus not a matter of memorization alone but of cultivating a sensibility for fabric behavior. When a sewist sees the diagonal slash of a twill weave symbol, they should anticipate durability and drape. When they read a cotton pictograph paired with a polyester percentage, they should predict ease of care and reduced shrinkage. When they encounter a stretch arrow annotated with recovery percentages, they should imagine how the garment will behave on the body, not just on the cutting table. To read these symbols fluently is to anticipate the life of the garment before a single seam is sewn.

In this sense, fabric behavior symbols invite the sewist into a kind of dialogue with the material. They say, "This cloth will move in this way, it will endure in this way, it will respond to your needle in this way." The sewist, in turn, chooses whether to heed or to experiment, guided but not constrained by the notation. It is in this exchange that patterns transcend their flatness, becoming not only technical instructions but invitations to material imagination.

## 3.2 Pre-Treatment and Preparation Symbols

Before fabric is ever cut, stitched, or pressed into a garment, it must often undergo preparation to ensure that the final product performs as intended. Patterns anticipate this by including a range of symbols that deal not with construction itself, but with what must be done to the fabric prior to construction. These symbols act as preventive medicine, guarding against shrinkage, distortion, or structural weakness that might otherwise ruin weeks of work.

One of the most significant of these pre-treatment indicators involves preshrinking. Natural fibers such as cotton, linen, and wool are notorious for shrinking when exposed to water and heat. To prevent finished garments from unexpectedly tightening after the first wash, fabric is often pre-washed or steamed before cutting. Symbols that indicate preshrinking requirements typically combine icons for temperature, time, and method. A wavy line paired with a thermometer may direct the sewist to wash in warm water, while a steam cloud icon signals the use of a pressing cloth and iron to shrink fibers in advance. Numbers alongside these symbols often specify duration, such as a thirty-minute soak, or temperatures, such as forty degrees Celsius. These marks are more than suggestions; they are integral to ensuring that the garment will maintain its intended dimensions once complete. Misinterpreting or ignoring a preshrinking symbol can lead to the heartbreak of a carefully sewn shirt rendered unwearable after a single wash.

Equally crucial in preparation are symbols for interfacing, the often invisible layer that provides structure to collars, cuffs, waistbands, and other areas requiring reinforcement. Interfacing symbols appear as shaded or patterned overlays on the pattern piece itself, mapping out where the interfacing must be applied. Distinctions are made between adhesive interfacing, often represented by a dotted texture or heat symbol, and sew-in interfacing, which may be indicated by dashed outlines without adhesive cues. Adhesive interfacing requires application with an iron, bonding directly to fabric with heat and pressure. Sew-in interfacing, by contrast, must be basted or stitched into place, offering a softer and more flexible reinforcement. The symbol tells the sewist not only which areas of the garment require reinforcement but also which technique to use, preventing the all-too-common mistake of using adhesive where sew-in is needed, or vice versa.

Stabilizers represent another layer of preparation, particularly in areas subjected to stress or intricate stitching. In embroidery, buttonholes, or delicate fabrics, stabilizer symbols may appear as shaded rectangles, crosshatching, or reinforced zones. They communicate where additional material should be applied to prevent fabric from puckering, stretching, or tearing under the needle. In a buttonhole, for instance, the stabilizer ensures that repeated buttoning and unbuttoning will not fray the cloth. In embroidery, it prevents dense stitching from distorting the base fabric. These symbols are critical in bridging the gap between design and durability. Without them, a garment may look pristine on completion day but quickly degrade under use.

Pre-treatment and preparation symbols, though often overlooked by beginners eager to get straight to cutting and sewing, are in truth the guardians of longevity. They acknowledge that fabric is a living material, one that changes under heat, moisture, and stress. By embedding these instructions into the pattern itself, designers ensure that the sewist respects the fabric's needs before attempting to shape it into a garment. The marks are small, but their significance is vast, standing between a garment that shrinks, warps, or collapses and one that holds its form for years.

## 3.3 Special Handling and Cutting Instructions

Once the fabric is properly prepared, the act of cutting introduces another set of challenges. Not all fabrics can be treated alike. Some have directionality in their fibers or surface texture, while others bear printed designs that demand alignment. Special handling and cutting symbols account for these realities, guiding the sewist through choices that affect both the look and function of the finished garment.

One of the most vital cutting symbols involves nap direction. Fabrics such as velvet, corduroy, and certain brushed wools possess a nap, a surface texture that reflects light differently depending on orientation. A nap symbol, often depicted as a directional arrow along the pattern layout, instructs the sewist to place all pieces consistently so that the nap runs in the same direction. If misread, garments made of napped fabric can appear patchy, with panels reflecting light unevenly as though from mismatched dye lots. The nap arrow ensures visual harmony, preserving the fabric's richness. In addition to nap, similar symbols exist for one-way designs, where printed motifs such as florals or stripes must face a single direction. These symbols warn the sewist to avoid rotating pattern pieces for efficiency at the expense of design coherence. A dress with flowers growing upright on the bodice but sideways on the skirt may be technically well-constructed yet aesthetically compromised, all because a symbol was ignored.

Cutting instructions also distinguish between single layer and double layer layouts. Most fabrics are folded double, with pattern pieces pinned and cut through both layers at once. However, delicate, bulky, or heavily patterned fabrics often require single layer cutting for precision. Symbols for single layer cutting are usually heavy arrows paired with notes such as "Cut 1" or outlines duplicated separately across the layout diagram. They tell the sewist to lay out fabric flat, cutting one piece at a time, even if it means more effort. Double layer symbols, by contrast, are lighter or paired with fold lines, signaling that mirrored pairs of pieces can be cut in one pass. These distinctions may seem technical, but they safeguard against subtle asymmetries that can ruin the balance of a garment. Cutting a plaid fabric on the double fold, for example, may shift lines slightly off, whereas cutting each piece singly ensures pattern alignment.

Mirror image requirements add yet another layer of complexity. Many garments demand left and right versions of the same piece, such as sleeves, bodice fronts, or pant legs. Mirror symbols indicate that pieces must be cut in pairs, reversed across a central axis. This is often shown with a mirrored outline or twin arrows facing each other. The symbol prevents the common error of cutting two identical left sleeves, leaving the sewist scrambling for extra fabric to correct the mistake. Mirror cutting is especially vital when fabric carries directional prints, because a motif pointing one way on the left side must be reversed symmetrically on the right. Without careful attention to these symbols, the final garment risks asymmetry, imbalance, or wasted material.

Together, nap arrows, single versus double layer indicators, and mirror image requirements represent the discipline of precision in cutting. They remind the sewist that fabric is not a neutral medium but one with texture, design, and direction that must be respected. These symbols are, in essence, a dialogue between the pattern drafter and the fabric itself, acknowledging that the cutting stage is as decisive as stitching in shaping the garment's success.

The larger lesson embedded in these symbols is that sewing is not merely about assembly but about foresight. A sewist who follows nap arrows preserves the harmony of fabric texture. One who honors single layer symbols avoids distortion. One who respects mirror indicators ensures balance. Each of these acts demonstrates attentiveness to detail, the hallmark of craftsmanship. These symbols, modest in size but profound in implication, transform fabric cutting from a perfunctory task into a stage of creative responsibility, where the integrity of the garment is either secured or compromised.

# Chapter 4: Hardware and Notion Placement Diagrams

*"The zipper installation symbol has undergone 23 documented revisions since 1925, each reflecting advances in fastener technology."*

## 4.1 Closure System Positioning Marks

The world of sewing is not limited to fabric alone. A garment may begin with cloth, but it rarely ends there. To be functional, clothing requires closures: the mechanisms that allow garments to open and close, to be put on and taken off, to remain secure on the body while permitting movement and comfort. Closure systems—zippers, buttons, hooks, snaps, magnets—are not mere afterthoughts but integral design elements. They dictate not only how a garment functions but also how it looks and feels. To guide the placement of these mechanisms, patterns employ specialized symbols, ensuring that the maker installs them with precision. These marks are small but indispensable, the visual cues that align technical necessity with aesthetic intention.

Among closure systems, the zipper holds a place of particular importance and complexity. Since its commercial breakthrough in the early twentieth century, the zipper has revolutionized garment construction, replacing laces, hooks, and rows of buttons with a single efficient fastener. Yet zippers are not monolithic. They come in many varieties—invisible, exposed, centered, lapped—and each type requires its own placement strategy.

Patterns distinguish between invisible and exposed zippers through variations in their symbols. An invisible zipper, designed to disappear into the seam, is often indicated by a fine dashed line with arrows terminating at the seam allowance, accompanied by small notches that denote where the zipper should begin and end. These subtle symbols remind the sewist to position the zipper coil directly on the seam line, hiding it completely when closed. By contrast, exposed zippers are marked with heavier lines, sometimes doubled, and symbols that emphasize the visible tape. These marks tell the sewist that the zipper is intended as a feature rather than something concealed, and must therefore be installed with equal parts precision and aesthetic care. The evolution of zipper symbols mirrors the evolution of zippers themselves, adapting to technological advances in coils, teeth, and insertion methods, and reflecting shifts in fashion from discretion to deliberate display.

Buttons and buttonholes form another essential closure system, and their placement is among the most symbolically dense aspects of a pattern. Unlike zippers, which require only alignment along a seam, buttons and buttonholes must be carefully spaced to ensure symmetry, comfort, and balance. Symbols for button placement appear as small circles or dots along a vertical line, while buttonholes are represented by elongated bars intersecting the line horizontally. These markings are not arbitrary. They follow spacing formulas that take into account the overlap of plackets, the stress points of the garment, and the desired aesthetic rhythm. For instance, a blouse may require evenly spaced buttonholes every seven centimeters, with additional reinforcement symbols at the bust or waist where strain is greatest. Jackets often feature a calculated overlap, where the button and buttonhole lines are offset to ensure the garment closes securely without gaping. These formulas, distilled into symbols, carry the weight of mathematical proportion. They ensure that buttons not only close the garment but also contribute to its harmony. A misread buttonhole mark can cause a cascade of issues: crooked plackets, mismatched overlaps, or garments that pull unevenly across the body. Thus, the small dots and bars of button placement are as much architecture as decoration.

Hooks, eyes, and snaps represent closure systems that, though smaller and often hidden, demand equal attention in their notation. Symbols for these fasteners typically appear as paired marks: a circle representing the hook, an adjacent cross for the eye, or twin dots for a snap's male and female parts. While modest, these marks carry high stakes. Placed incorrectly, a hook and eye at the top of a zipper will fail to align, leaving the garment gaping. A snap misaligned by even a few millimeters may not fasten securely, or worse, cause distortion in delicate fabrics. These symbols therefore act as precise coordinates, ensuring that closures align perfectly under stress. In patterns for lingerie, bridal wear, or couture garments, such marks may appear in dense sequences, guiding the placement of multiple tiny fasteners that together bear the weight of fit and design.

In recent decades, magnetic closures have entered the repertoire, especially in accessories such as handbags and outerwear. Their symbols often incorporate concentric circles or stylized magnet icons, indicating both polarity and placement. Because magnetic closures rely on perfect alignment between two halves, their positioning marks are critical. Misplaced symbols can result in closures that attract unevenly, compromising both function and appearance. The inclusion of magnetic symbols reflects the ongoing expansion of pattern notation to accommodate technological innovation, much as earlier generations adapted to zippers or snaps.

What unites these diverse closure symbols is their dual role as both technical instructions and design indicators. A zipper symbol does not merely tell the sewist where to place a fastener; it also communicates whether the designer intends the closure to vanish or to stand out as a statement. A line of button symbols is not just a practical fastening system but also a visual rhythm that shapes how the garment is perceived. Snap, hook, and magnetic symbols may seem utilitarian, but they signal the designer's choices about subtlety, security, and ease of wear. In every case, the placement marks bridge the gap between mechanical necessity and aesthetic judgment.

To interpret closure system marks effectively, the sewist must develop an awareness of proportion and alignment. For zippers, this means ensuring that seam allowances, notches, and endpoints match the symbol precisely, preventing distortion when the garment is zipped. For buttons and buttonholes, it requires measuring distances carefully, respecting the formulas embedded in the pattern, and sometimes adjusting spacing to suit individual body proportions. For hooks, snaps, and magnets, it demands precision down to the millimeter, since small errors can have outsized consequences. These tasks are not glamorous, but they distinguish skilled craftsmanship from careless work. The symbols act as a discipline, a silent overseer reminding the maker that closures are as integral to a garment's success as seams and darts.

The evolution of closure symbols also reflects broader shifts in fashion history. The early twentieth century saw an explosion of button placement formulas, as men's tailoring codified conventions for lapels, cuffs, and waistcoats. The zipper, initially marketed as a novelty, required entirely new symbols to guide installation, with revisions proliferating as nylon coils and invisible zippers entered the market. The rise of ready-to-wear garments pushed button and snap placement toward industrial uniformity, while couture houses continued to guard proprietary symbols for elaborate hook-and-eye systems. Today, the addition of magnetic closure symbols marks yet another stage in this ongoing dialogue between technology, design, and notation. Each new closure system requires its own grammar, and patterns expand their lexicon accordingly.

To the beginner, closure marks may seem like minor details—dots, lines, circles, crosses scattered along a placket or seam. To the professional, they are the culmination of centuries of adaptation, mathematical precision, and technological evolution. They represent a promise: that the garment will open and close as intended, that it will balance on the body without gaping, that it will align perfectly at points of stress. Misread or ignored, they cause frustration, wasted fabric, and garments that fail to function. Interpreted correctly, they allow closures to vanish seamlessly or shine as intentional design features.

In every buttonhole bar, zipper arrow, or snap dot lies a fragment of history and innovation. They remind us that garments are not static objects but dynamic systems, designed to move, flex, and fasten around the human form. The symbols ensure that these systems operate as intended, transforming the abstract lines of a pattern into clothing that can be lived in. To master them is to join a long tradition of makers who understand that the smallest marks often carry the greatest weight.

## 4.2 Reinforcement and Support Elements

Clothing must not only close neatly but also withstand the forces of wear, movement, and time. This is where reinforcement and support elements come into play, often unseen by the wearer yet critical to the garment's durability and fit. Pattern symbols for these elements guide the sewist in placing invisible structures that give garments their strength and shape. The vocabulary of reinforcement is as rich as that of closures, for it covers everything from the rigid architecture of boning to the controlled elasticity of stretch fabrics and the subtle directional stitching that prevents distortion.

Boning channel symbols are among the most specialized in this category, particularly common in corsetry, structured gowns, and certain costumes. These symbols usually appear as elongated rectangles or parallel lines along seams or panels, sometimes annotated with numbers that indicate flexibility ratings. A lightweight synthetic boning might be marked differently than a steel variety, each carrying distinct implications for comfort and silhouette. These symbols tell the sewist not only where to insert the boning but also what level of rigidity is expected. A gown requiring dramatic shaping through the waist will use high-flex steel or spiral boning, while a lighter summer bodice may call for plastic boning that bends more easily. Misinterpreting these symbols can compromise the entire garment: inserting overly stiff boning in a design meant for gentle shaping results in discomfort, while too soft a reinforcement leaves the garment collapsing under its own weight. The symbols act as guardians of balance, ensuring that structure supports rather than overwhelms.

Elastic application marks represent another essential system of reinforcement. Unlike boning, which resists movement, elastic facilitates controlled expansion and contraction, offering comfort without sacrificing shape. Symbols for elastic application often take the form of shaded zones, arrows stretching across a length of fabric, or annotations specifying tension percentages. For example, an annotation of "75%" may instruct the sewist to stretch the elastic to three-quarters of its relaxed length when attaching it to the fabric. These numerical guides are vital because elastic must be distributed evenly to avoid puckering or distortion. In waistbands, cuffs, lingerie, and athletic wear, the proper application of elastic ensures both secure fit and long-term recovery. A waistband stretched inconsistently will dig into the skin on one side and sag on the other. The tension percentage indicators embedded in symbols translate the mathematics of stretch into a simple instruction, allowing the sewist to achieve uniformity without guesswork.

Stay-stitching, though less visible than boning or elastic, is no less important in garment reinforcement. It involves stitching along curved or angled edges before final construction, preventing fabric from stretching out of shape during handling. Symbols for stay-stitching often appear as fine directional arrows along seam curves, showing both the path and the direction in which the stitching should be applied. The direction is not arbitrary. Stitching from shoulder to bust or from waist to hip follows the natural grain of the fabric, locking threads in place against distortion. If reversed, the fabric may warp, causing gaping or uneven seams. These symbols thus act as preventive measures, ensuring that garments hold their intended contours through every stage of assembly. To ignore them is to invite the slow creep of distortion that only reveals itself after hours of work, when the garment suddenly refuses to lie flat.

Together, boning channels, elastic application, and stay-stitching paths represent the silent infrastructure of clothing. They do not dazzle the eye like decorative elements, nor do they serve the obvious function of closures. Yet without them, garments lose their shape, stretch unevenly, or collapse under stress. Their symbols guide the sewist in weaving strength and resilience into the very fabric of design. Every rectangle marking a boning channel, every arrow signaling stay-stitching, every percentage beside an elastic zone embodies the invisible craft that transforms fragile fabric into enduring clothing.

## 4.3 Decorative Hardware Integration

If reinforcement elements serve the skeleton of a garment, decorative hardware provides its adornment. These symbols represent the ways in which metal, trim, and appliqué integrate into fabric not just for function but for beauty. The placement of such features must be precise, for they are as unforgiving as they are striking. A rivet set slightly off balance, a grommet misaligned, or a trim stitched unevenly can mar the design beyond repair. Patterns therefore use a specialized set of symbols to guide the integration of these embellishments with accuracy.

Rivets, grommets, and eyelets share a long history in sewing, from reinforcing workwear to embellishing high fashion. Their placement symbols usually appear as small circles, sometimes annotated with diameter measurements to indicate size. A rivet may be marked with a filled circle, while a grommet or eyelet might be represented by an open circle, reminding the sewist that fabric will be pierced to create an opening. These distinctions matter greatly, as the wrong size or position can weaken the fabric instead of strengthening it. In denim jeans, rivets placed at stress points like pocket corners prevent tearing; in corsetry, rows of grommets provide channels for lacing; in decorative garments, eyelets may serve purely aesthetic purposes, framing embroidery or lace. The symbols not only pinpoint placement but often dictate sequence, ensuring that hardware is added at the proper stage of construction when the garment can still be easily handled.

Decorative trim attachment lines provide another layer of visual instruction. These lines often run parallel to seam lines or edges, marked with specific notations that indicate layering sequences. A double line may signal that trim should be applied atop fabric after construction, while a dashed line may indicate insertion between seam layers. In elaborate designs, trims may overlap in sequences, requiring multiple symbols to show which lies above or below. This symbolic layering is crucial in garments where lace, ribbon, or braid create depth and texture. A misplaced trim line can result in bulk where none was intended or a flattened appearance where dimension was desired. By following the symbols, the sewist can replicate the designer's vision of interplay between cloth and decoration.

Appliqué positioning guides extend this symbolic system into the realm of fabric-on-fabric decoration. Symbols for appliqué may appear as shaded shapes or outlines on the pattern, corresponding to the motif's intended placement. Additional notations distinguish between adhesive application, represented by textured shading or heat icons, and stitched application, marked by dashed outlines indicating sewing paths. These distinctions are critical for durability and appearance. An adhesive appliqué, suitable for lightweight decorative accents, will not withstand the repeated stress of laundering without reinforcement, while a stitched appliqué provides permanence but alters the drape of the base fabric. By reading the symbols, the sewist chooses not only where to place the appliqué but how to secure it in a way that balances beauty and longevity.

Decorative hardware integration symbols reveal the intersection of craft and artistry. They ensure that embellishments enhance rather than compromise the garment. A rivet placed precisely at a stress point is both reinforcement and ornament. A trim stitched in the correct sequence adds richness without bulk. An appliqué positioned according to its symbol sits in perfect harmony with the garment's lines. These small marks carry immense weight, encoding the difference between elegance and awkwardness, between refinement and error.

The history of these symbols mirrors fashion's changing relationship with decoration. In earlier centuries, trims and appliqués were often hand-applied without standardized notation, relying on the judgment of artisans. With industrialization, patterns needed to codify these placements to ensure consistency across production. Rivets, once purely functional reinforcements in workwear, became fashion statements in jeans, demanding precise symbols for their placement. Grommets moved from utility in corsetry to decorative motifs in modern streetwear. Each shift required an expansion of the symbolic lexicon, allowing patterns to communicate not just construction but ornamentation.

For the sewist, reading these symbols is both technical and creative. It requires accuracy in execution, ensuring that each embellishment aligns with its designated position. At the same time, it invites reflection on the role of decoration in design. These marks remind the maker that garments are not only protective shells but canvases for expression, where rivets glint, trims ripple, and appliqués tell stories. In every circle, line, or shaded motif lies the possibility of turning fabric into art.

# Chapter 5: Seam Construction and Finishing Techniques

*"French seams require seven distinct symbols to fully communicate their construction process—making them the most symbol-dense technique in sewing notation."*

## 5.1 Basic Seam Assembly Indicators

Seams are the backbone of garment construction. Every piece of fabric, no matter how carefully cut or prepared, only becomes a garment when joined to another piece. The seam is therefore both a structural and aesthetic element: it holds fabric together, determines how the garment fits, and often contributes to its overall appearance. Because of this central role, sewing patterns use a wide array of symbols to guide seam assembly. These symbols go beyond simple instructions to stitch here or there. They communicate the orientation of fabric, the direction in which seams must be pressed, and the distribution of ease across seams. To read them properly is to unlock the grammar of garment construction, translating flat cloth into a functional, wearable form.

One of the first seam assembly indicators that a sewist encounters is the distinction between right sides together and wrong sides together. Fabrics are rarely neutral; one side is intended to be public, the other hidden. The difference may be subtle—a sheen on one side, a print, or even a slight texture—but it matters profoundly to the finished garment. Patterns signal this orientation through specific symbols. Right sides together, the most common configuration in construction, is typically indicated by solid lines meeting at a seam, sometimes reinforced with paired arrows that show the fabric faces folding inward. This symbol tells the sewist that the seam allowance will be hidden inside the garment, producing a clean outer finish. Wrong sides together, used in techniques such as flat-felled seams or certain decorative applications, is marked differently, often by broken or dotted lines paired with outward-facing arrows. These symbols remind the sewist that the seam allowances will remain visible on the outside unless finished separately. Confusing these symbols can mean producing a seam that either exposes raw edges where they should be concealed or hides decorative stitching that was meant to be shown. Thus, they are more than orientation marks; they are decisions about the relationship between garment interior and exterior, between structure and display.

Once fabric orientation is established, the next step is pressing, an often underestimated process that determines the durability and drape of the seam. Symbols for seam pressing direction usually appear as arrows laid along seam lines, showing the way seam allowances should be pressed. A single arrow pointing to one side indicates pressing allowances together in that direction, while opposing arrows signal pressing allowances open. This distinction shapes how the garment behaves. Seams pressed open lie flat and distribute bulk evenly, common in tailored garments. Seams pressed to one side create additional strength and thickness, useful in jeans or casual wear. Alongside these directional arrows, patterns sometimes include temperature indicators, represented by stylized iron icons with dots or numbers corresponding to heat levels. These marks are particularly important when working with delicate fabrics such as silk or synthetics that can scorch or melt under high heat. By pairing pressing direction with temperature guidance, these symbols transform an invisible step of construction into a precise technical act, ensuring both safety and quality.

Ease gathering represents another essential component of seam assembly notation. Not all seams join fabric of equal length. Sometimes a longer piece must be eased into a shorter one, creating gentle shaping without obvious gathers. Sleeve caps, for example, require the sleeve head to be eased into the armhole, distributing excess length smoothly so the sleeve curves over the shoulder without puckering. Symbols for ease gathering appear as series of small tick marks, shaded sections, or lines annotated with ratios. A ratio of two to three, for instance, might indicate that two units of fabric length must be eased into three units of seam, guiding the sewist in distributing fullness evenly. These marks are not decorative but mathematical. They encode the calculations of pattern drafters who have determined exactly how much fabric must be eased to achieve the intended fit. Misinterpreting them results in sleeves that pucker or bodices that sag, undermining the garment's silhouette.

The role of ease distribution symbols is to transform complex mathematics into simple visual guides. Rather than requiring the sewist to measure and calculate, they provide direct cues: here is where you must gather slightly, here is where you must release. When used properly, they ensure that fullness disappears invisibly into the garment, shaping it without calling attention to itself. This ability to hide complexity behind simplicity is one of the great virtues of sewing notation. A cluster of marks may look minor on a paper pattern, but in practice it controls the delicate balance between comfort, movement, and form.

These three categories of seam assembly symbols—orientation, pressing, and ease—work in concert to guide construction from the first stitch to the final press. Right-sides-together marks tell the sewist how to align fabric pieces. Pressing arrows guide the aftercare of each seam, ensuring bulk is controlled and drape maintained. Ease ratios distribute fabric fullness invisibly, sculpting the garment to the body. Each symbol has its own role, but together they create a continuous chain of instructions, ensuring that every seam is strong, smooth, and aligned with the designer's intent.

Their significance becomes even clearer when one considers what happens if they are misread. Sewing wrong sides together instead of right sides together might not be immediately noticeable, but by the time the garment is turned, it may reveal exposed seams that cannot be hidden without major reconstruction. Pressing seams in the wrong direction may seem trivial until the garment refuses to lie flat, creating lumps or stiffness. Misinterpreting ease gathering symbols can ruin a sleeve or distort a bodice, errors that often cannot be undone without unpicking and starting again. In each case, the symbols are not optional details but safeguards against failure. They are the visual manifestation of experience, capturing the lessons of countless sewists and drafters who discovered, often through error, what must be done for seams to succeed.

The history of seam assembly symbols also tells us much about the evolution of garment making. In earlier centuries, seam construction knowledge was passed orally or through apprenticeship, with little reliance on standardized notation. The rise of printed patterns in the nineteenth century demanded that these instructions be codified, creating a vocabulary of marks that could be read by sewists of varying skill levels. By the twentieth century, as mass-produced garments became standard, seam symbols grew increasingly precise, incorporating pressing instructions, ease ratios, and even heat settings. They evolved in step with fabrics themselves: synthetics required careful temperature management, while new designs demanded more sophisticated shaping techniques. Each addition to the symbolic lexicon expanded the ability of patterns to communicate subtlety and precision.

For the modern sewist, fluency in these symbols is as important as skill with a needle. They are not supplementary notes but integral parts of construction, guiding every stage from cutting to finishing. The best way to appreciate their value is to observe them in practice. Take the construction of a simple blouse. The pattern shows the front and back bodice pieces with right-sides-together seam symbols along the shoulders. Arrows instruct the sewist to press these seams open, ensuring the neckline lies smoothly. Along the sleeve cap, ease gathering symbols guide the distribution of extra length, allowing the sleeve to curve without puckering. Each symbol intervenes at a critical moment, shaping the garment's final appearance. Without them, the sewist would be left to guess, risking a blouse that fits poorly or looks unfinished. With them, the garment takes on a professional finish, even in the hands of a beginner.

Ultimately, seam assembly symbols embody the philosophy of sewing notation itself. They distill complex processes into accessible cues, democratizing knowledge that once belonged only to trained artisans. They allow garments to be reproduced with accuracy across time and space, whether in a Paris atelier or a suburban sewing room. And they remind us that the strength and beauty of a garment depend not only on design or fabric but on the invisible joints where pieces meet. To master these symbols is to master the art of construction at its most fundamental level, ensuring that every seam is not just a line of stitches but a carefully considered act of design.

## 5.2 Complex Seam Engineering Symbols

Not all seams are equal in complexity. Some exist merely to join two pieces of fabric together, while others are feats of engineering, designed to combine durability, comfort, and visual refinement in a single line of stitching. Complex seam constructions often demand several layers of preparation, reinforcement, and finishing, and because of this, their notation systems are equally intricate. Patterns that include these seams cannot rely on a single symbol; instead, they use sequences of marks that break down each stage of the process, ensuring clarity and precision.

One of the most important of these advanced constructions is the flat-felled seam, often found in jeans, workwear, and shirts where durability is paramount. A flat-felled seam encloses raw fabric edges within multiple folds, creating a seam that is both strong and neat. The symbols for this seam usually consist of parallel lines of varying thickness, accompanied by annotations that specify the width of each fold. Numbers might be added along the symbol, indicating that one side of the seam must be folded at a quarter inch, while the other is folded at a half inch, creating an overlapping lock. These specifications ensure that the seam lies flat without excess bulk. Without the width indicators, a sewist might guess incorrectly, producing a seam too thick to press properly or too weak to withstand tension. The flat-fell seam symbol is thus a visual shorthand for a sequence of actions: fold, stitch, fold again, and topstitch, all compressed into a concise diagram.

Another sophisticated seam finish is the bound seam, which involves enclosing the raw edges of fabric within bias tape. This technique not only protects the fabric from fraying but also creates a decorative interior finish, often used in unlined jackets or couture garments where the inside is expected to look as polished as the outside. Symbols for bound seams typically appear as double lines with angled markers showing the orientation of the bias tape. The angle matters greatly, since bias tape stretches diagonally across the grain, allowing it to curve smoothly around edges. An incorrect angle would cause the tape to warp, buckle, or pull against the seam. By reading the angled application indicators, the sewist ensures that the binding conforms to the seam's shape while maintaining flexibility. In some patterns, shading or crosshatching within the symbol distinguishes between visible decorative binding and hidden structural binding, further clarifying the designer's intent.

Perhaps the most symbolically dense of all engineered seam constructions is the welt seam pocket, a staple of tailored jackets and trousers. Unlike a simple patch pocket, a welt pocket involves slicing into the body fabric, folding back edges, and inserting a pocket bag behind a reinforced opening. The symbols for welt pocket seams often combine dashed cutting lines, rectangles indicating the welt position, and reinforcement marks at corners. Small triangles or crosses may appear at the ends of the opening, instructing the sewist to reinforce these points with short bar tacks. These symbols are essential because a welt pocket is unforgiving: once fabric has been cut, errors cannot be concealed. The reinforcement indicators in particular are crucial, since the pocket opening endures significant stress every time the wearer inserts a hand. By following the placement and reinforcement marks, the sewist not only creates a clean, professional pocket but ensures its longevity.

Complex seam symbols, then, are not merely guides to construction but compact systems that condense multiple steps into one notation. They tell the sewist exactly where to fold, how much to trim, where to insert reinforcements, and how to align decorative finishes. They also reveal the philosophy of sewing notation itself: that clarity of symbols allows complex engineering to be accessible even to those who may not have years of training. A flat-felled seam, a bound seam, or a welt pocket may each require multiple steps, but with well-designed symbols, the process becomes reproducible, efficient, and precise.

## 5.3 Seam Finishing and Edge Treatments

If engineered seams represent the architecture of construction, seam finishes are the polish that ensures garments endure and look refined. Edges of fabric, once cut, are vulnerable to fraying, distortion, and wear. Finishing techniques address this vulnerability, and their symbols record how each edge should be treated. From industrial serging to delicate Hong Kong finishes, these marks instruct the sewist not only in what to do but in how many threads, layers, or strips are required to produce a professional result.

The serger, or overlock machine, dominates modern edge finishing. Its symbols are often represented by multiple parallel lines or loops along the edge of a pattern piece, annotated with thread counts such as three-thread, four-thread, or five-thread finishes. These distinctions are not trivial. A three-thread overlock finish provides a lightweight edge finish suitable for knits, while a five-thread version incorporates a safety stitch, combining seam construction and finishing in one pass. The symbols communicate which type of serger stitch the designer intends, preventing the sewist from using a stitch too weak for the fabric or unnecessarily bulky for a lightweight garment. In industrial production, where efficiency and fabric economy are critical, misinterpreting these thread count symbols could compromise entire production runs.

A more refined alternative appears in the Hong Kong seam finish, beloved in couture and high-end ready-to-wear garments. This technique involves encasing the raw edge of a seam allowance with a bias strip, creating a clean, colorful finish inside the garment. Symbols for Hong Kong finishes typically show parallel lines with a diagonal overlay, representing the bias strip. Additional markers may indicate the width of the bias, ensuring consistency in application. These symbols remind the sewist that the finish is not purely functional but also decorative, contributing to the internal beauty of the garment. In unlined jackets, where the inside is often as visible as the outside, these finishes demonstrate craftsmanship. Without the symbols, a sewist might default to a simpler overlock, losing the opportunity for refinement intended by the designer.

Simpler still, yet still symbolically distinct, are edge treatments such as pinking, binding, or turned-and-stitched finishes. Pinking, the practice of cutting fabric edges with serrated shears to reduce fraying, is often symbolized by zigzag lines along the edge of a pattern piece. Though it may appear rudimentary, the symbol signals that the designer expects a lightweight, non-bulky finish rather than a stitched edge. Bound edges, in contrast, are shown through double lines or shaded overlays, similar to bound seam symbols but applied to raw edges of single layers rather than joined seams. Turned-and-stitched finishes, common in heirloom sewing and fine shirting, are represented by curved arrows and dashed fold lines, showing where the edge should be folded under before stitching. These variations, though small on paper, produce dramatically different results in practice, affecting both durability and appearance.

Seam finishing symbols also carry cultural significance, reflecting the differing priorities of industrial versus couture sewing. In factory garments, serger symbols dominate, emphasizing efficiency, speed, and cost reduction. In couture or bespoke garments, Hong Kong, bound, or turned finishes appear more frequently, embodying values of craftsmanship and refinement. The symbols themselves embody these values, telling the sewist not just how to finish a seam but what philosophy of garment-making is being enacted.

The power of these symbols lies in their ability to ensure consistency. A seam finished with a three-thread serge looks different from one finished with a Hong Kong binding, and without clear notation, two sewists following the same pattern might produce wildly different results. By encoding edge treatments into patterns, designers preserve their vision across multiple hands and contexts. The symbols transform finishing from an afterthought into a planned, integral part of garment design.

For the sewist, mastering seam finishing symbols is not only about technical competence but also about aesthetic sensitivity. Reading them fluently means anticipating how the inside of the garment will look, how it will feel against the skin, and how it will endure repeated use. A serger mark promises efficiency, a Hong Kong line promises elegance, a pinked edge promises simplicity. Each symbol carries not just an instruction but an implication, a vision of what the garment should embody.

# Chapter 6: Three-Dimensional Shaping Symbols

*"Couture garments can contain up to 47 different shaping symbols in a single pattern piece, each controlling how flat fabric transforms into sculptural form."*

## 6.1 Dart Manipulation and Control

No matter how beautiful a fabric may be, it begins as a flat plane. The human body, by contrast, is curved, dynamic, and full of subtle variations. Sewing exists to reconcile these two realities, transforming two-dimensional cloth into three-dimensional form. Among the most powerful tools for achieving this transformation are darts, those small folds of fabric that, once stitched, give garments contour and fit. The role of darts is so fundamental that sewing notation has developed an elaborate vocabulary of symbols to control every nuance of their placement, size, and direction. These marks are not casual; they are precise guides to shaping, ensuring that garments not only fit but flatter.

Curved dart symbols are among the most expressive in this system. While a basic dart is represented by two straight converging lines meeting at a single apex point, curved dart symbols introduce arcs that suggest more complex shaping. These symbols communicate that the dart should not be sewn as a straight line but as a gentle curve, sculpting the fabric in a way that follows the natural contours of the body. They are especially common in areas where the body does not lend itself to linear adjustments, such as over the bust or across the hip. The apex point itself may be marked with additional annotations, indicating whether the dart should end exactly at the fullest point of the curve or stop short to create a smoother transition. These variations are subtle but critical. A dart sewn too close to the bust apex creates an unnatural point, while one ending slightly before the apex produces a rounded, natural silhouette. Symbols that communicate apex variations therefore prevent common mistakes, ensuring that the shaping looks elegant rather than forced.

Double-pointed darts, also known as fisheye darts, expand on this principle by shaping fabric at both ends. These darts are typically drawn as elongated diamonds on the pattern, with each end tapering to a point. Symbols associated with them often include small annotations for take-up measurements, which specify how much fabric should be folded into the dart. A take-up of one centimeter at each end produces a gentle contour, while larger take-ups create more dramatic shaping. Double-pointed dart symbols frequently appear in dresses, jackets, and fitted garments where waist suppression and bust contouring must be achieved simultaneously. Reading these symbols accurately allows the sewist to sculpt the garment to the body's natural curves without creating bulk or distortion. Their presence on a pattern signals not only complexity but refinement, for they require careful stitching and precise interpretation to achieve the intended effect.

Dart conversion symbols take the principle of shaping even further, showing how darts may be transformed into pleats, gathers, or style lines. On a pattern, these conversions are often represented by arrows radiating from the dart point, accompanied by notations that indicate how the excess fabric should be redistributed. A pleat conversion symbol, for example, may replace the converging dart lines with parallel fold lines, turning a shaping device into a design feature. Gather conversion symbols often use clusters of small lines or shading to indicate that the dart excess should be eased into gentle fullness, softening the garment's silhouette. Style line conversions are more complex, showing the dart excess rotated into a seam that becomes part of the garment's overall design, such as a princess seam. These symbols empower the sewist to understand that darts are not fixed but fluid, capable of being reimagined into alternative forms of shaping that combine function with creativity.

What makes dart symbols particularly important is their ability to communicate three-dimensional intent through two-dimensional notation. A cluster of lines on paper represents not only where fabric should be stitched but how it will behave in space. This is no small feat. The difference between a curved dart, a double-pointed dart, and a dart converted into a pleat may look minor on paper but produces entirely different garments in reality. These symbols are therefore acts of translation, converting the designer's vision of form into a language the sewist can execute. They condense geometry, anatomy, and aesthetics into compact marks that guide the transformation of cloth into body-conscious design.

In couture contexts, dart manipulation becomes even more symbolically dense. A single bodice piece may contain curved dart symbols at the bust, double-pointed darts along the waist, and conversion arrows showing how excess is rotated into princess seams. Each mark carries meaning, and the sewist must read them as a system rather than in isolation. Couture patternmakers use these symbols not only to achieve fit but to sculpt the garment into an artistic form, balancing tension and release across the fabric. A dart extended into a style line becomes part of the visual rhythm of the design, while a double-pointed dart refined by take-up measurements creates subtle waist suppression invisible to the eye yet felt in the fit. The symbols act as a blueprint for this sculptural vision, guiding the sewist to reproduce the designer's intent with precision.

Historically, the codification of dart symbols reflects the growing sophistication of garment design. Early darts were rarely formalized; they were often improvised adjustments made directly on the fabric during fitting. With the rise of printed patterns, symbols became necessary to communicate these shaping techniques consistently. Over time, the symbols grew more complex, introducing curved lines, apex notations, and conversion arrows as fashion demanded more intricate silhouettes. The twentieth century saw an explosion of dart manipulation in both home sewing and couture, with symbols proliferating to keep pace with innovation. Today, patterns may contain entire families of dart symbols, each corresponding to a different technique of shaping, and each demanding careful reading.

For the sewist, learning to interpret dart manipulation symbols is not only about technical skill but also about developing an eye for form. These marks teach the maker to anticipate how fabric will curve, fold, or release, and to visualize the garment in three dimensions even while working on a flat surface. To read a curved dart symbol is to imagine how the bust will appear under cloth. To follow a double-pointed dart indicator is to anticipate how waist and hip will be contoured. To interpret a conversion symbol is to envision how excess can be transformed into pleats that ripple or seams that elongate the silhouette. This ability to project from symbol to form is one of the great gifts of sewing notation, a bridge between paper and body, between idea and execution.

Errors in reading dart symbols are among the most common pitfalls for beginners. Misplacing the apex point or stitching to the wrong end can distort the garment's fit dramatically. Ignoring take-up measurements in double-pointed darts may result in garments that pull awkwardly across the waist. Misinterpreting conversion arrows may turn a design intended as a smooth style line into an unintended bulk of fabric. These mistakes reveal the high stakes of dart notation: small marks with large consequences. Yet they also underscore the importance of mastering this symbolic language, for with mastery comes freedom. Once the sewist understands darts not as rigid rules but as flexible tools encoded in symbols, they gain the ability to alter, adapt, and innovate, transforming garments to suit unique bodies and personal visions.

Ultimately, dart manipulation and control symbols represent the artistry of garment shaping distilled into a visual system. They show how to bend flatness into curve, how to suppress fullness into contour, how to release control into design. They are symbols that sculpt, guiding the fabric into harmony with the body it will embrace. To master them is to hold the key to three-dimensional sewing, where cloth ceases to be a surface and becomes a form.

## 6.2 Pleat Formation and Specifications

While darts sculpt fabric into localized curves, pleats create rhythm, depth, and volume across broader expanses. They are architectural features of clothing, simultaneously functional and decorative. To form them correctly, symbols guide the sewist through a choreography of folding and pressing, marking where fabric must be doubled back on itself, how much material is consumed in each fold, and in which direction the pleats should fall. These marks are not arbitrary; they are codified to ensure consistency, for even slight miscalculations in pleat depth or spacing can disrupt the garment's balance.

Box pleats are among the most recognizable types, creating symmetrical folds that open outward from a central point. On patterns, box pleats are typically represented by paired arrows pointing in opposite directions, flanking a central fold line. Alongside these arrows, numbers often indicate depth and spacing, such as two centimeters per fold or five centimeters between pleats. These measurements ensure that the pleats align evenly across the garment, whether in a skirt, a uniform, or a tailored coat. Without symbols clarifying depth and spacing, the sewist would be left to guess, risking uneven pleats that throw off both the drape and the symmetry of the garment. The symbols act as visual equations, translating geometry into cloth, ensuring that each fold consumes exactly the right amount of fabric and falls at the intended interval.

Knife pleats, by contrast, create directional flow, with all folds pressed to the same side. Symbols for knife pleats often consist of a series of parallel arrows, each pointing in the direction of the fold. Accompanying these arrows may be ratio indicators, such as two-to-one or three-to-one, specifying how much fabric is consumed relative to the finished width. For instance, a two-to-one ratio means that twice as much fabric is gathered into the pleat as is visible on the garment's exterior, producing sharp, crisp folds. The ratio is crucial because it controls the garment's fullness and mobility. A skirt with knife pleats marked at three-to-one will move with more dramatic flare than one marked at two-to-one. Symbols prevent inconsistency by encoding this mathematical relationship directly onto the pattern, ensuring that every pleat conforms to the intended rhythm.

Inverted pleats combine aspects of both box and knife pleats, folding inward so that fullness is hidden beneath the garment's surface. Symbols for inverted pleats often resemble mirror-image arrows converging toward a central line, annotated with underlay fabric requirements. These underlay notations specify how much fabric must be hidden beneath the fold to allow the pleat to open comfortably. Without sufficient underlay, the pleat strains when the garment is worn, pulling awkwardly and distorting the design. Too much underlay, however, creates unnecessary bulk. The underlay indicators embedded in pleat symbols ensure that the balance is correct, that the pleat opens gracefully without compromising comfort or silhouette.

The symbolic system of pleats demonstrates the precision with which patterns manage fabric volume. A line of arrows and numbers may appear modest on paper, but it encodes the consumption of fabric, the spacing of folds, and the direction of movement. For the sewist, these marks are indispensable, transforming what could be guesswork into a repeatable, reliable process. They embody the principle that beauty in clothing often emerges from disciplined structure, with symbols acting as the architects of rhythm and proportion.

## 6.3 Gathering and Fullness Distribution

Pleats provide structure through precise folds, but gathering creates softness through controlled irregularity. Gathering allows fabric to be drawn together into small, even ripples, creating volume and texture while maintaining flexibility. Symbols for gathering communicate where stitching must be placed, how much fabric is drawn into a smaller space, and how that fullness is distributed across the garment.

Gathering stitch placement is typically indicated by parallel dashed lines running along the edge of a pattern piece, annotated with ratio specifications. A one-to-two ratio, for example, signals that one unit of finished length must accommodate two units of fabric, producing gentle ripples. A one-to-three ratio produces denser, more dramatic gathers. These symbols prevent uneven distribution, which would otherwise cause bunching in some areas and flatness in others. When interpreted correctly, they ensure that fullness is spread evenly, allowing a sleeve head to sit smoothly into an armhole or a skirt to flow gracefully around the waist. Gathering symbols thus encode mathematical precision into what appears to be a loose, organic effect, proving again that notation transforms unpredictability into repeatable design.

Cartridge pleats represent a more specialized form of fullness distribution, historically used in ecclesiastical robes, Tudor gowns, and Victorian skirts. Unlike ordinary gathers, cartridge pleats create deep, rounded folds that stand away from the body, achieved by stitching fabric into tight, evenly spaced points. Symbols for cartridge pleats often appear as grids of dots or paired markers, each corresponding to a stitch point. Historical variations exist, with earlier symbols emphasizing decorative spacing and later ones focusing on structural support. These marks guided seamstresses in creating consistent spacing, ensuring that the pleats rose like architectural columns rather than collapsing into uneven folds. Even today, in costume construction and couture, cartridge pleat symbols retain this importance, directing the sewist to transform large expanses of fabric into sculptural volume.

Smocking preparation adds yet another layer to the symbolic vocabulary of fullness. Smocking gathers fabric into decorative grids, embroidered over to create elasticized panels that expand and contract with movement. Preparation symbols for smocking usually appear as arrays of dots arranged in geometric grids across a pattern piece. These dots mark the points where fabric must be gathered with preliminary stitches, setting the stage for the embroidery that follows. Without these guides, smocking would be nearly impossible to execute consistently, as the spacing of gathers directly determines the elasticity and appearance of the finished panel. Different grid patterns yield different smocking effects, from honeycomb textures to lattice designs. Symbols for these grids ensure accuracy, standardizing what would otherwise be an inexact, laborious process.

The unifying theme across gathering, cartridge pleats, and smocking is control of fullness. Each technique manipulates excess fabric, but the symbols define how that manipulation should occur—whether in gentle ripples, architectural folds, or elasticized grids. Without these marks, the sewist would struggle to achieve balance, producing garments that sag, bulge, or distort. With them, even complex distributions of fabric can be managed with confidence, transforming excess into elegance.

Together, pleat and gathering symbols reveal how sewing notation mediates between flat fabric and three-dimensional form. They translate geometry, mathematics, and design intent into compact visual cues. They ensure that volume is not accidental but deliberate, whether expressed in the symmetry of box pleats, the sharpness of knife pleats, the hidden depth of inverted pleats, the softness of gathers, the grandeur of cartridge pleats, or the elasticity of smocking. For the sewist, fluency in these symbols unlocks the ability to shape fabric into rhythm, movement, and form, turning raw material into garments that flow, drape, and sculpt the body with precision.

# Chapter 7: Professional Tailoring and Couture Symbols

*"Savile Row tailors employ 89 proprietary symbols unknown outside their workshops, some dating back to the 1800s."*

## 7.1 Canvas and Interfacing Architecture

When one steps into the world of professional tailoring and couture, the symbolic language of sewing expands into its most intricate and guarded forms. Unlike mass-produced patterns designed for home sewists, couture blueprints are closer to architectural drawings than simple instructions. They are layered with symbols that map out hidden structures, components that give garments their sculptural quality and longevity. At the heart of this symbolic vocabulary lies canvas and interfacing architecture, the foundation of bespoke jackets, coats, and dresses. These markings guide not only where hidden reinforcements should be placed but also how they should be shaped, stitched, and eased into the garment so that the final product holds its form yet moves naturally with the body.

The most emblematic of these symbols are those for hymo canvas, a type of haircloth traditionally woven from horsehair blended with wool or other fibers. Hymo canvas is prized for its ability to provide structure without stiffness, forming the skeleton of tailored garments. Placement diagrams for hymo canvas are usually shaded overlays on pattern pieces, often annotated with zones for different densities of pad stitching. Pad stitching itself is a technique where small diagonal stitches, invisible on the garment's surface, secure the canvas to the fabric while shaping it into curves. Symbols for pad stitching zones may take the form of diagonal hatching or angled arrows, with variations in density indicating stitch frequency. For example, tighter hatching near the lapel roll line signals denser pad stitching, necessary to train the fabric to curve gracefully when folded. Looser hatching toward the lower front suggests lighter stitching, maintaining structure without excessive rigidity. These diagrams are not decorative abstractions; they are precise maps, translating centuries of tailoring experience into shorthand that ensures garments roll, curve, and drape exactly as intended.

Beyond the canvas, professional tailoring employs chest pieces—multi-layered assemblies that reinforce the upper torso of jackets and coats. Chest piece shaping symbols are complex, often combining contour lines, arrows, and notations for ease. They communicate not only the placement of different materials—such as layered felts, domettes, or light canvas—but also how those materials must be eased into the garment to produce subtle shaping. The ease requirements indicated by these symbols are crucial. A chest piece cannot simply be cut to match the fabric; it must be slightly smaller or larger in certain areas to allow the fabric to swell or compress as the garment is worn. Arrows may show where ease should be distributed, while curved contour lines indicate how the layers must be trimmed or stretched to follow the natural line of the chest. Without these symbols, a sewist might apply reinforcement too rigidly, producing a jacket that looks boxy and unnatural. With them, the maker achieves a chest that appears full yet soft, with just enough spring to suggest vitality rather than stiffness.

Shoulder reinforcement, another critical element of tailoring, has its own set of symbols. The shoulder is a point of immense stress in garments, carrying weight and determining balance. Symbols here often indicate the application of twill tape or stay tape, narrow strips of woven material that prevent stretching and distortion. On a pattern, these may appear as parallel lines running along shoulder seams, annotated with specifications for tape width. Some patterns also include arrows indicating the direction in which the tape should be applied, ensuring that it supports the grain of the fabric rather than fighting against it. A half-inch twill tape applied in the wrong direction can distort an entire jacket, throwing off the hang of the sleeve and the line of the lapel. The symbols ensure that reinforcement aligns with both fabric behavior and body movement, stabilizing the garment where it matters most.

The symbolic language of canvas, chest pieces, and shoulder reinforcement reflects the philosophy of tailoring itself: garments must have both structure and suppleness. The diagrams are not rigid prescriptions but nuanced maps, guiding the sewist to combine firmness with flexibility. They demand an understanding that fabric is alive, that it stretches, swells, and responds to climate and wear. By embedding ease requirements, pad stitching zones, and directional reinforcements into symbols, patterns communicate not only where materials should be placed but how they must interact with the body and with each other.

Historically, these symbols emerged in the private workshops of master tailors, guarded as trade secrets. On Savile Row, in Naples, in Parisian ateliers, each house developed its own notation system, often indecipherable to outsiders. A diagonal hatch might mean pad stitching in one workshop but indicate underlay in another. Apprentices spent years learning to interpret these marks, not only memorizing their meanings but also absorbing the philosophy behind them. In many cases, the symbols were deliberately cryptic, serving as a barrier to prevent competitors from stealing methods. What to the untrained eye looked like an arbitrary scratch on a pattern was, in fact, a signifier of generations of knowledge about shaping fabric into living form.

With the advent of industrial tailoring and published manuals, some of these symbols became more standardized, but the heart of couture remains proprietary. Even today, a jacket drafted by a Savile Row cutter may contain symbols that would puzzle a home sewist, designed not for mass comprehension but for those initiated into the house's language. This exclusivity reinforces the aura of bespoke garments, where part of the value lies in the hidden structures and the secret marks that map them.

For the sewist approaching these symbols from the outside, learning to interpret them is both technical and philosophical. To read a hymo canvas placement diagram is to understand that structure must vary across a garment, heavier at the lapel, lighter at the hem. To decode chest piece shaping marks is to realize that ease is not an accident but a calculated allowance, inserted deliberately to mimic the natural swell of the body. To follow shoulder reinforcement lines is to grasp that stability is not uniform but must align with grain and stress. Each symbol becomes a key, unlocking not only instructions but insights into the logic of tailoring.

Errors in reading these symbols can be catastrophic. A chest piece applied without ease may cause the front of a jacket to bulge or pull. Pad stitching executed outside its marked zone may distort the roll of a lapel. Shoulder tape applied incorrectly can cause sleeves to hang awkwardly, ruining the garment's balance. These mistakes illustrate the high stakes of tailoring notation, where precision is not a luxury but a necessity. The symbols act as guardrails, preventing errors that even skilled sewists might otherwise make when working without the invisible hand of tradition.

Yet the importance of these marks goes beyond technical correctness. They embody an aesthetic philosophy: that the most beautiful garments are shaped not only by visible design but by hidden architecture. The wearer may never see the pad stitching zones, the chest ease indicators, or the twill tape reinforcements, yet they feel their effects in the garment's comfort, poise, and longevity. Symbols preserve this invisible craft, ensuring it can be reproduced and transmitted, even when the knowledge itself is too subtle to explain fully in words.

To master canvas and interfacing symbols is to step into the mindset of a tailor, seeing fabric not as flat cloth but as a material with potential for sculptural life. Each shaded zone, each arrow, each annotated measurement whispers centuries of accumulated understanding, inviting the sewist to participate in a tradition that values patience, precision, and artistry. In these marks, the hidden skeleton of couture is revealed, a silent architecture that makes garments not just clothing but enduring works of craft.

## 7.2 Hand-Stitching Technique Indicators

In the realm of professional tailoring and couture, machines play their part, but the soul of a garment often lies in hand-stitching. These stitches, though small and subtle, achieve effects no industrial process can replicate. Because hand-sewing leaves little margin for error, patterns and tailoring diagrams employ a sophisticated lexicon of symbols to guide their execution. Each mark corresponds to a specific stitch, its length, spacing, and placement—all of which are critical to maintaining consistency across a garment.

One of the most frequently encoded techniques is the fell stitch, valued for its ability to produce a nearly invisible finish. The symbol for the fell stitch often appears as staggered diagonal dashes along a seam line, indicating how the needle should pass through fabric layers at a shallow angle. These symbols frequently include directional cues, showing whether the stitches must slant left or right, depending on the seam's position in the garment. The invisible finish requirement is implied by the spacing and density of the marks, with tighter groupings suggesting greater subtlety. When correctly interpreted, the symbol reminds the sewist that the needle should just skim the outer layer, anchoring the seam without letting thread show on the surface. In couture workshops, apprentices spend months perfecting the fell stitch precisely because its success is judged not by what can be seen, but by what cannot. Symbols encode this demand for discretion, distilling centuries of couture discipline into a few careful lines.

Equally important are pick stitch spacing guides, which combine function with ornament. The pick stitch, a short running stitch that shows as tiny, evenly spaced dots on the fabric surface, is used both decoratively and to reinforce seams. On patterns, its symbol often appears as a dotted line with annotations that dictate spacing, such as two millimeters or three millimeters between each stitch. This spacing is not arbitrary but part of the aesthetic rhythm of the garment. In a tailored lapel, evenly spaced pick stitches highlight the edge, framing it with understated elegance. If the spacing drifts, the line wavers, undermining the sharpness of the tailoring. The symbols act as a metronome for the hand, reminding the sewist to maintain consistency across the entire edge. In luxury tailoring, where visual harmony is everything, these pick stitch symbols transform what could be irregular handwork into a refined signature of craftsmanship.

Catch stitch indicators round out this symbolic trio, guiding the placement of hem and lining attachments. The catch stitch creates small diagonal crisscrosses on the inside of a garment, anchoring fabric layers without allowing thread to pull taut. Symbols for this technique typically appear as alternating diagonal lines crossing over a seam or hem edge, often accompanied by arrows to show direction of work. These diagrams tell the sewist to form a loose but secure connection, preventing hems from rolling outward or linings from sagging. Because catch stitches must flex slightly with the garment, their symbols often emphasize balance: not too tight, not too loose. Interpreted properly, they ensure that hems remain invisible from the outside while remaining resilient through wear. Misread, they result in puckered hems or unsecured linings, mistakes that compromise both comfort and elegance.

Together, fell stitch, pick stitch, and catch stitch symbols form a cornerstone of tailoring notation. They remind us that couture is not built solely on bold gestures but on small, controlled actions repeated with care. These marks are not just technical guides but guardians of discipline, ensuring that each hand stitch—whether invisible, decorative, or functional—serves its purpose with precision. For the sewist, fluency in these symbols is a rite of passage, the difference between amateur improvisation and professional mastery.

## 7.3 Pressing and Shaping Tool Marks

If stitching is the skeleton of a garment, pressing is the sculptor's hand, shaping fabric into curves, edges, and volumes that endure through wear. Professional tailoring symbols therefore extend beyond stitching to the pressing stage, encoding where tools such as tailor's hams, clappers, sleeve boards, and point pressers should be applied. These tools allow fabric to be molded three-dimensionally, setting seams and shaping contours in ways that cannot be achieved with stitching alone.

Symbols for ham curves often appear as arched lines or semi-circular overlays across curved pattern sections such as bust darts or hip seams. These marks indicate that the area must be pressed over a tailor's ham, a rounded cushion designed to mimic body contours. The symbols may also include directional arrows showing how the curve should be shaped during pressing—whether to emphasize outward fullness or to smooth fabric inward. Without these indicators, a sewist might press a curve flat on a standard ironing board, inadvertently distorting the garment's natural shaping. Interpreting ham curve symbols ensures that pressing complements stitching, turning darted fabric into lifelike form.

Clapper usage points are another specialized notation, typically represented by rectangular symbols or short perpendicular lines crossing seam allowances. A clapper, a block of hardwood used to set seams, requires pressure applied directly after steaming, locking fibers into place as they cool. The symbols highlight zones where a sharp, crisp edge is essential, such as lapels, trouser creases, or tailored hems. They may also be accompanied by annotations specifying duration of pressure, reminding the sewist that timing is critical. Too little pressure, and the seam relaxes into softness; too much, and the fabric risks losing resilience. These marks are a subtle reminder that pressing is as much about restraint as force, and that precision matters even in seemingly mechanical steps.

Sleeve board and point presser application zones round out the repertoire, ensuring that narrow or awkward areas of the garment receive appropriate treatment. Symbols for sleeve board usage often appear as elongated ovals aligned with sleeve patterns, indicating where pressing must occur to maintain cylindrical shape without flattening. Point presser symbols, by contrast, are often sharp triangles or wedge shapes annotated along collar points, cuffs, or corners. They tell the sewist to use the narrow wooden tool to press seams open in confined spaces, preventing bulk and ensuring clean angles. These notations may seem minor, but their impact is profound. A collar pressed with a point presser lies sharp and symmetrical, while one pressed carelessly may look blunt or uneven.

The inclusion of pressing and shaping tool symbols in tailoring patterns underscores a critical truth: pressing is not an afterthought but an integral part of construction. These marks codify what might otherwise be left to intuition, ensuring consistency across garments and makers. They acknowledge that fabric, once stitched, must be trained to hold its new shape, and that this training requires specialized tools applied with precision. The symbols are visual reminders that shaping is a dialogue between needle and iron, between stitch and steam, between human hand and resistant fiber.

Historically, these pressing symbols developed in tandem with the refinement of tailoring techniques in the nineteenth and early twentieth centuries. As tailored garments grew more structured, the role of pressing tools became central, and so did the need to encode their use in patterns. Just as canvas placement diagrams preserve structural knowledge, pressing marks preserve shaping knowledge, ensuring that garments emerge from construction not as flat assemblages of seams but as sculptural forms.

For the sewist, reading these symbols opens a deeper understanding of tailoring philosophy. They convey that the garment is not finished when stitched; it is finished when pressed into life. A ham curve symbol is a reminder to respect the body's natural roundness. A clapper mark instructs patience, teaching that fabric must cool under weight before it will hold an edge. A point presser symbol insists on precision, telling the sewist that even the smallest corners deserve attention. These are not optional flourishes but fundamental acts of craftsmanship.

When hand-stitching indicators and pressing tool marks are considered together, they reveal the holistic nature of couture notation. Symbols map every stage of the process, from invisible stitches to invisible shaping, guiding the sewist through a choreography where nothing is left to chance. They encode discipline and tradition, preserving knowledge that might otherwise be lost in the shift from apprenticeship to printed instruction. For those who learn to read them, they offer entry into a world where garments are not merely constructed but sculpted, their beauty arising as much from hidden craft as from visible design.

# Chapter 8: Industrial and Mass Production Symbols

*"A single misinterpreted symbol in factory production can result in 10,000 defective garments before detection—costing manufacturers up to $500,000."*

## 8.1 Assembly Line Sequencing Markers

While couture symbols protect traditions of handcraft, industrial symbols serve an entirely different mission: speed, uniformity, and control on a massive scale. In a factory environment where thousands of garments must be produced each day, symbols become the language that coordinates people, machines, and materials with clockwork efficiency. Their role is not only to ensure that garments are constructed correctly but also to track time, labor costs, and quality. These marks are therefore less about artistry and more about orchestration, functioning as the notation of an industrial symphony where every worker and every machine must know its place in the score.

One of the most ubiquitous forms of industrial notation is the operation number code. Each stage of garment construction, from attaching a pocket to finishing a hem, is assigned a unique numerical identifier. These codes appear on factory patterns, work tickets, and digital systems, guiding operators to perform tasks in precise sequence. Alongside the numbers are time allocations, often measured in seconds, reflecting how long each operation is expected to take. For example, the code "034 –

Attach waistband – 28s" tells the operator not only what to do but also how quickly it should be done. Symbols linked to these codes may include arrows showing stitching paths, icons denoting machine type, or abbreviations for specific seam finishes. Interpreting these codes correctly is essential, for in a production line, efficiency is measured not in minutes but in fractions of a minute. A misread code can cause bottlenecks, disrupt workflow, and inflate costs. Unlike couture, where time is elastic, industrial sewing depends on exact coordination, and the symbols of operation numbers provide the structure.

Closely tied to these sequencing codes are bundle ticket symbols, which act as passports for groups of garment pieces as they move through the factory. A bundle ticket is a strip of paper or card attached to a stack of cut fabric pieces, recording every operation completed on them. Symbols on these tickets indicate not only which steps have been performed but also where quality checkpoints occur. A circle or stamp icon might show that a seam must be inspected for alignment before proceeding, while a star may denote a checkpoint for stitch density. These symbols ensure accountability, for each operator signs or punches the ticket after completing their operation. If a defect is later discovered, the ticket reveals exactly where in the line the problem occurred. In mass production, where garments pass through dozens of hands, these symbols provide traceability, protecting both efficiency and quality.

The evolution of bundle ticket symbols reflects the increasing complexity of production management. In early factories, workers relied on foremen for verbal instructions, but as volumes grew, visual systems became necessary to track progress at scale. Today, bundle tickets may incorporate barcodes or QR codes alongside traditional printed symbols, linking physical garments to digital management systems. Yet the fundamental role remains the same: to communicate quickly, without ambiguity, what has been done and what remains, ensuring that no operation is skipped and no defect goes unnoticed.

Modular production systems, which replace long assembly lines with small teams handling groups of operations, have their own symbolic language. In modular systems, symbols often represent roles rather than operations, indicating which team member is responsible for which part of the garment. These may appear as initials, color-coded icons, or schematic diagrams showing task distribution within a module. Arrows might depict how partially assembled garments move between workers, ensuring that tasks are balanced and downtime is minimized. Unlike traditional line systems, modular symbols emphasize flexibility, as teams must adapt to variations in demand and design. Interpreting them requires not only reading the marks but understanding the philosophy of collaborative workflow they embody.

Together, operation codes, bundle tickets, and modular symbols form the backbone of industrial sequencing notation. They translate the chaos of thousands of garments, machines, and workers into a controlled process where every step is measured, recorded, and verified. Their precision reflects the stakes: in a factory, a single misinterpreted symbol does not ruin one garment but potentially thousands, multiplying errors into costly recalls or reputational damage. The rigor of these symbols therefore mirrors the rigor of the production environment itself, where efficiency, consistency, and accountability matter more than artistry.

To understand the power of assembly line sequencing markers, consider a factory producing denim jeans. The process may involve more than fifty discrete operations, from stitching back yokes to attaching rivets. Each operation has a code, a time allocation, and a quality checkpoint. The symbols tell the operator whether to use a chain stitch machine or a lockstitch machine, whether to fold seam allowances inside or outside, and where to inspect stress points. The bundle ticket ensures that no stack of jeans progresses without verification, while modular diagrams balance workload among teams. Without these symbols, the factory would descend into disorder, with inconsistent garments, wasted fabric, and missed deadlines. With them, thousands of jeans emerge virtually identical, each pair a testament to the power of visual notation in mass production.

Unlike the secrecy of couture, industrial symbols are designed for clarity and universality. They must be legible to workers of varied backgrounds, often across language barriers, and therefore rely heavily on standardized icons and numbers. Yet they share with couture notation the same underlying principle: that symbols can preserve knowledge, reduce ambiguity, and guide hands with precision. Where couture symbols preserve artistry, industrial symbols preserve efficiency. Both are expressions of human ingenuity, adapting the language of marks to the demands of their context.

For the sewist outside the factory world, these symbols may seem foreign, even cold. But understanding them reveals another dimension of sewing's symbolic grammar, one where garments are not unique expressions but units of production. Reading operation codes, bundle tickets, and modular diagrams is to glimpse the logic of mass manufacturing, where each mark carries the weight of thousands of repetitions. They remind us that garments are not only crafted but produced, and that symbols are the invisible infrastructure making such scale possible.

## 8.2 Quality Control and Inspection Points

In the controlled chaos of industrial garment production, symbols are not limited to construction and sequencing. Just as vital are those that signal inspection, marking the exact places and conditions under which garments must be checked before moving to the next stage of the line. These symbols are the silent guardians of consistency, ensuring that thousands of garments leave the factory floor identical in size, color, and durability. Without them, the precision of operation codes and bundle tickets would collapse under the weight of unnoticed errors.

Critical measurement points form the backbone of inspection notation. On industrial patterns, these points are indicated by crosses, circles, or triangles placed at specific coordinates—across chest, waist, hip, sleeve length, or inseam. Each point is paired with tolerance ranges, often expressed numerically on accompanying documentation. For instance, a chest measurement may be marked as "52 cm ± 0.5 cm," meaning that the finished garment must measure between 51.5 and 52.5 centimeters at that location. These tolerance symbols ensure uniformity without demanding impossible perfection. Workers on the inspection line use them as checkpoints, measuring garments with tape measures or calibrated rulers against the annotated points. A misinterpreted or ignored measurement symbol may result in hundreds of garments that deviate from specification, creating costly returns or rejections by retailers. The marks, therefore, are not suggestions but strict boundaries within which industrial consistency is maintained.

Thread tension check symbols add another layer to this inspection framework. Industrial machines run at extraordinary speeds, and thread tension can shift subtly during production, affecting seam quality. Symbols for tension checks often appear as small loop icons or zigzag markers printed near seam lines, paired with annotations showing acceptable stitch density. Inspectors reading these marks know to pull slightly on seams, ensuring that thread neither breaks nor hangs too loosely. Adjustment guides may be incorporated, showing which dial or lever on the machine corresponds to the correct correction. These notations prevent catastrophic issues like seam failure, which can appear only after garments reach consumers. By embedding thread tension checks into patterns and production paperwork, factories create a visual routine of verification, integrating quality into the flow of work rather than leaving it to chance.

Color matching indicators bring yet another dimension to quality control, especially in garments composed of multiple components or produced across different facilities. Symbols for color matching often take the form of shaded blocks, half-tone squares, or coded icons linking components together. They tell inspectors that the collar must match the body fabric, that linings must be consistent across batches, or that panels cut from different dye lots must not show perceptible difference. In high-volume production, fabrics may come from multiple suppliers, and even minor shifts in dye saturation can create jarring inconsistencies. Color matching symbols prevent these errors by requiring inspectors to compare components under standardized lighting conditions, often specified directly in the notation. A mark may indicate "D65" lighting, meaning daylight-simulated bulbs must be used, ensuring consistency across inspection sites. These symbols are vital because the human eye can be deceived by ambient conditions; codified marks provide an objective system to counteract subjectivity.

Together, measurement points, tension checks, and color matching symbols create a network of quality assurance embedded directly into the production process. They ensure that garments are not only assembled quickly but also meet the rigorous standards of buyers and consumers. Each symbol represents a checkpoint, a pause in the rush of production where precision takes precedence over speed. In this way, inspection notation protects both the manufacturer and the customer, ensuring that efficiency does not override quality.

## 8.3 Packaging and Shipping Preparations

Once garments have passed inspection, their journey is not yet complete. For industrial production, the final stage is packaging and shipping, where symbols continue to play a critical role. These marks guide how garments should be folded, hung, protected, and presented, ensuring that when they arrive at retailers, they look pristine and uniform. A poorly folded garment or incorrectly hung jacket may not ruin its construction, but it undermines presentation, reducing perceived value and increasing handling costs for stores. Symbols for packaging translate logistical needs into clear visual cues, coordinating factory workers who must prepare thousands of items for shipment each day.

Fold line symbols are among the most common in this stage. These marks, often represented by dashed or dotted lines across pattern layout diagrams or production sheets, indicate exactly where garments should be folded for retail presentation. The symbols may be annotated with numbers showing sequence, ensuring that folding is consistent across all units. For instance, a shirt pattern may include fold line marks across the sleeves and torso, instructing workers to fold sleeves inward before folding the body in half. Such uniformity ensures that garments fit neatly into packaging, stack efficiently, and present a consistent appearance when unpacked. Without these fold indicators, variations in worker technique would result in uneven stacks, misaligned collars, or packaging that bulges awkwardly. Symbols impose discipline, ensuring every garment leaves the factory as though folded by the same invisible hand.

Hanger placement marks address another critical element of packaging, particularly for suits, coats, and dresses shipped on hangers rather than folded. These symbols often appear as small hook icons or rectangles along shoulder seams, annotated with dimensions for hanger width and weight distribution. They instruct workers where hangers must be inserted and how garments should balance to avoid distortion during transport. For delicate fabrics, additional marks may show where padding should be applied to hangers to prevent shoulder dimpling. These notations ensure that garments arrive at retail locations ready to hang directly on racks, free from unsightly creases or stretching. In an industry where first impressions drive sales, hanger placement symbols protect the garment's dignity in transit.

Tissue paper and plastic cover symbols provide further protection during packaging. Tissue paper insertion points are often indicated by shaded zones or icons resembling folded sheets, showing where tissue must be placed to prevent creasing or friction between layers. Plastic cover specifications, represented by outlined garment silhouettes with shading or annotations, dictate whether garments must be enclosed individually or grouped in sets. They may also include thickness requirements, ensuring adequate protection during long-distance shipping. These marks ensure that the garment's journey from factory to warehouse to store is one of preservation, guarding against dust, moisture, and mechanical damage.

Packaging symbols are often overlooked in discussions of sewing notation, yet they are as integral to industrial production as construction or quality control. They embody the reality that a garment is not finished when sewn, nor even when inspected, but only when it reaches the consumer in saleable condition. These marks guide the final choreography of preparation, ensuring that garments survive the stresses of transport while still embodying the precision and uniformity that industrial systems demand.

The philosophy of packaging notation mirrors that of industrial production as a whole: efficiency, uniformity, and predictability. Folding lines, hanger icons, tissue overlays, and plastic cover diagrams transform the messy realities of shipping into a standardized process where nothing is left to interpretation. For the sewist studying these symbols, they reveal the hidden labor of logistics, showing that garments are not only constructed but also choreographed for presentation, carrying symbols that govern their final appearance before reaching the consumer's eye.

# Chapter 9: Digital Pattern and Smart Textile Symbols

*"By 2025, augmented reality sewing apps will introduce an estimated 200 new dynamic symbols that change based on fabric selection and skill level."*

## 9.1 CAD Software Symbol Libraries

The transition from paper to screen has not diminished the importance of sewing symbols; instead, it has multiplied their complexity and expanded their role. In the digital era, pattern-making software no longer limits itself to static marks drawn on paper. Within computer-aided design systems, symbols are dynamic, parametric, and layered, designed to adapt instantly to changes in measurement, design, or construction method. They are not just guides for human interpretation but also data points that communicate directly with machines, printers, and even augmented reality platforms. Understanding these digital symbol libraries requires a new literacy, one that blends traditional sewing knowledge with fluency in software logic.

One of the most transformative innovations in digital patterning is the development of parametric symbols. Unlike static lines and arrows on paper, parametric symbols are programmed to adjust automatically when a pattern is resized or altered. Consider the example of a dart symbol in a CAD program. In a paper pattern, resizing a garment would require the drafter to manually recalculate dart take-up, redraw lines, and reposition the apex. In a digital environment, however, the dart symbol is parametric: its length, angle, and endpoint shift automatically as the body measurements change, maintaining proportional accuracy without manual recalculation. Grainline arrows, seam allowances, pleat depth indicators, and even notches are all now defined as parametric objects, capable of responding to adjustments in real time. This innovation ensures consistency, reduces human error, and accelerates design. Yet it also requires the sewist to understand that symbols are no longer fixed but algorithmically defined. To misinterpret or override a parametric symbol is to risk breaking the logic of the pattern, resulting in inconsistencies when pieces are assembled.

Layer-based symbol systems represent another dimension of digital notation. In CAD programs, patterns can be divided into layers, each containing different categories of information—structural lines, notches, annotation symbols, grading data, and construction guides. These layers can be toggled on or off, allowing the user to focus on one aspect of the pattern at a time. Symbols within this system are not only visual guides but also organizational markers, helping manage complexity. For example, a designer might hide all finishing symbols to concentrate on shaping symbols, or isolate grainline and fold indicators to prepare for cutting layouts. In collaborative environments, different teams—patternmakers, graders, quality engineers—may work on different layers, each relying on the integrity of its symbol system. The layer-based approach prevents visual clutter while ensuring that no information is lost. However, it introduces its own symbolic discipline: sewists must be aware of which layer a symbol belongs to, or risk missing critical instructions when exporting patterns for printing or machine cutting. The symbols here are not simply marks but part of a file's architecture, embedded into the very structure of digital patterning.

Perhaps the most striking innovation in CAD symbol libraries is the advent of animation symbols. Traditional symbols are static, instructing the sewist what to do but not how movement should unfold. Animation symbols, however, contain embedded sequences that visually demonstrate construction steps. For instance, a pleat symbol in an advanced CAD program might be linked to an animation that shows fabric folding inward, step by step, until the pleat is secured. A dart indicator might unfold into a short clip showing how the excess fabric is stitched and pressed toward the side seam. These animation symbols are dynamic teaching tools, bridging the gap between abstract notation and lived technique. They are especially valuable for beginners or for distributed production environments where training is difficult to provide in person. Instead of relying solely on written manuals, factories and classrooms can use animation symbols to standardize construction knowledge across multiple locations.

The presence of animation symbols also points toward the future integration of augmented reality into sewing practice. Already, some CAD platforms are experimenting with QR-linked or app-synced symbols that can project animated instructions directly onto fabric through a mobile device or smart glasses. A sewist following an invisible zipper symbol, for instance, might scan the code and watch a holographic overlay demonstrate the insertion technique directly on the garment. In this sense, the boundary between symbol and instruction dissolves, as symbols evolve from static shorthand into interactive portals. To understand them is not only to read a mark but to activate a sequence of knowledge embedded within digital space.

The rise of CAD symbol libraries also transforms the role of standardization. On paper, variation in symbol style between publishers was tolerable, as most sewists could adapt. In digital environments, inconsistency can cause software incompatibilities, breaking automated grading or cutting routines. As a result, international efforts are underway to unify digital sewing symbol libraries across platforms. Standards ensure that a parametric seam allowance symbol defined in one program can be read correctly in another, or that animation symbols linked to pleat formation are universally recognizable. This global alignment mirrors earlier historical moments when industrial sewing required common vocabularies. The difference now is that the stakes are not only human comprehension but also machine interpretation.

For the sewist or designer navigating CAD environments, learning to read these digital symbols is akin to acquiring a new language. Where once a grainline arrow was a simple printed line, it is now a parametric object tied to databases of fabric properties. Where once a cluster of notches indicated ease distribution, it is now an animated sequence showing how fullness should be stitched and pressed. Where once a pattern was static, it is now layered, dynamic, and connected to broader networks of production. This shift demands a mindset that sees symbols not as fixed marks but as living, responsive elements within a digital ecosystem.

The implications extend far beyond the screen. Because CAD patterns feed directly into automated cutters, digital printers, and even robotic sewing machines, symbols serve as instructions not only for humans but for machines. A parametric notch ensures that cutting heads mark fabric accurately; a layer-based symbol determines whether seam lines are cut or only drawn; an animation symbol may soon be linked directly to robotic arms executing pleats or darts. In this sense, symbols have moved from being interpretive aids to becoming executable code. To misread them is not just to misunderstand instructions but to disrupt entire production systems.

The future of CAD sewing symbols promises even greater expansion. As smart textiles—fabrics embedded with sensors, conductive threads, or adaptive fibers—become more common, symbols will need to represent not only structural and aesthetic information but also electronic pathways, heating zones, or stretch-response areas. A parametric symbol might indicate where conductive yarn must be inserted, adjusting automatically if the garment is resized. A layer-based symbol might control which parts of the textile respond to temperature changes. Animation symbols might demonstrate not only how to sew but also how the garment behaves when powered on. These developments suggest that sewing symbols are evolving into a hybrid language, one that unites design, construction, and technology into a single visual grammar.

For the practitioner today, the challenge is to stay literate as symbols evolve. Mastery of parametric adjustments allows one to trust that resizing will not distort construction. Understanding layers ensures that complexity remains manageable. Recognizing animation symbols opens access to dynamic, interactive instruction. Each of these competencies transforms the way sewing knowledge is applied in the digital age. They preserve the continuity of tradition—grainlines, darts, pleats—while embedding it in a system designed for speed, precision, and adaptability.

Ultimately, CAD software symbol libraries reveal the trajectory of sewing notation itself. From medieval guild ciphers to industrial bundle tickets to digital animation icons, the story is one of adaptation to context. Symbols endure because they are efficient, because they compress knowledge into marks, and because they allow that knowledge to travel across hands, machines, and now even realities. To understand parametric, layered, and animated symbols is to recognize that the language of sewing has become not only visual but algorithmic. It is to see that the future of garments lies not only in fabric but in the marks that tell us how fabric should behave.

## 9.2 Smart Fabric Integration Markers

The twenty-first century has expanded the role of textiles far beyond warmth and modesty. Fabrics today are not merely passive materials; they are active participants in technology. Wearable electronics, illuminated textiles, and biometric garments all rely on careful planning and precise construction. To accommodate this transformation, sewing symbols have evolved into systems that guide not only the placement of seams and darts but also the integration of circuits, sensors, and energy pathways. These smart fabric markers represent a dramatic shift: the merging of tailoring traditions with electronic engineering.

Conductive thread pathway symbols are at the heart of this integration. On a digital pattern, these often appear as bold lines or arrows overlaid on seams or garment panels, sometimes differentiated from structural lines by color coding or unique textures. Unlike grainlines or seam allowances, these symbols indicate the flow of electrical current. Arrows show the direction of conductivity, while annotations specify whether the thread carries power, data, or ground. In more advanced systems, thickness indicators may accompany the symbol, representing resistance levels and the durability required for repeated flexing. Without these symbols, conductive pathways risk being misaligned or cut during sewing, breaking the circuit and rendering the garment nonfunctional. For sewists venturing into smart textiles, learning to read and respect conductive thread symbols is as crucial as respecting grainlines in traditional tailoring.

Beyond the threads themselves, symbols now exist to represent LED placement grids. Wearable illumination requires not only aesthetic positioning but also reliable routing of power. On patterns, LED grids are represented as arrays of small circles or squares, each linked by fine lines to show circuit continuity. These are often accompanied by power routing indicators, such as triangles or battery icons, clarifying where energy enters and exits the grid. Placement precision is critical: too close, and LEDs create harsh hotspots of light; too far, and the illumination appears uneven. Symbols resolve this by encoding spacing ratios, ensuring consistent distribution. They also account for the limitations of fabric: grids may be flexible, but they must not distort when worn, and symbols help anticipate how LEDs will shift across curves and seams.

Sensor integration points add yet another layer to this symbolic system. As biometric monitoring becomes more common, garments incorporate sensors that track heart rate, temperature, posture, or muscle activity. Symbols for sensors often take the form of concentric circles or square targets placed at specific body zones, such as the chest, wrist, or spine. Accompanying annotations may include calibration requirements or sensitivity ranges, ensuring that the sensor is positioned where it can collect accurate data. For example, a chest-mounted heart rate sensor must align closely with the sternum, and its symbol may include arrows or grids that help the sewist orient it correctly. Misinterpretation here does not merely produce aesthetic flaws; it compromises the garment's technological function. These symbols are therefore both technical and biomedical, bridging the gap between fashion and health sciences.

The development of smart fabric integration symbols illustrates how sewing notation has become a multidisciplinary language. Where once marks communicated only fabric behavior, now they must encode electrical flow, illumination geometry, and biological accuracy. For the sewist, mastering these symbols is both a technical and creative challenge, requiring sensitivity to aesthetics and functionality alike. The symbols remind us that garments are no longer static objects but interactive systems, woven into the rhythms of movement, light, and data.

## 9.3 3D Printing and Laser Cutting Notations

If smart fabrics represent the fusion of textiles with electronics, 3D printing and laser cutting represent the fusion of textiles with digital fabrication. These technologies allow garments to be cut, engraved, or even partially manufactured by machines guided directly by digital files. Their symbols, therefore, differ from traditional marks, functioning not only as human-readable guides but also as machine-readable instructions. They encode the parameters that determine how lasers interact with material, how printed elements flex or anchor, and how hybrid constructions combine both digital and manual methods.

Laser power setting symbols are among the most technical. Patterns prepared for laser cutting include marks that indicate not only cut lines but also engraving or scoring instructions. These are often differentiated by line weight, texture, or annotation, with specific symbols representing wattage or speed. A solid red line might indicate a through-cut at a designated power level, while a dashed blue line might indicate a light etching pass. The symbols ensure that the machine interprets the file correctly, preventing fabric from being scorched or undercut. For sewists, these marks are critical because different materials—cotton, polyester, leather, or synthetics—require different power settings to achieve clean cuts. A misread symbol can ruin an entire batch of fabric panels, or worse, create safety hazards. The precision of these symbols transforms laser cutting from a risky experiment into a predictable, repeatable process.

Three-dimensional printed element attachment points extend the symbolic vocabulary further. In hybrid garments where rigid or flexible printed components are combined with fabric, patterns use markers to indicate where these elements should be anchored. These may appear as geometric icons—hexagons for rigid pieces, spirals for flexible ones—annotated with dimensions or tolerance requirements. Flexibility zones are often marked with shading or curved arrows, signaling areas where the printed component must bend with the body rather than resist movement. For example, a printed exoskeleton panel on a jacket might include symbols showing that the shoulder region must flex to allow arm rotation, while the torso remains rigid for structural support. These notations ensure that 3D printed parts integrate seamlessly with fabric, enhancing rather than restricting wearability.

Hybrid construction symbols tie these systems together, showing how traditional and digital methods overlap. These symbols often appear as layered icons, combining classic sewing marks such as seam allowances with digital fabrication notations like laser power codes. For instance, a seam line might be overlaid with a laser symbol, indicating that the fabric edge is to be sealed by laser instead of stitched. Or a pleat indicator might include an attachment point icon, signaling that the fold will be stabilized by a printed clip rather than traditional stitching. These hybrid symbols communicate that construction is no longer bound to a single discipline but draws from multiple technologies. They remind the sewist and technician alike that modern garments are assemblages of processes, each requiring its own symbolic guide.

The introduction of 3D printing and laser cutting notations marks a profound shift in the philosophy of sewing symbols. Traditionally, symbols mediated between designer and sewist, encoding human actions. In the digital fabrication era, symbols also mediate between humans and machines, encoding parameters that must be executed by software and hardware. This dual role makes them both more powerful and more demanding, requiring literacy across multiple fields. For the maker, interpreting these symbols is to stand at the intersection of craft and code, where fabric and filament, seam and laser, needle and algorithm converge.

Together, smart textile markers and digital fabrication notations reveal the future trajectory of sewing symbols. They show how a language once confined to paper has expanded into interactive, programmable, and hybrid systems. Conductive thread pathways, LED grids, and biometric sensor symbols transform garments into living technologies. Laser power settings, 3D printed attachment points, and hybrid construction icons turn sewing patterns into digital blueprints, bridging human creativity with machine precision. In mastering these symbols, the sewist embraces a future where garments are not only worn but experienced, not only stitched but engineered, not only fashioned but coded.

# Chapter 10: Specialty Techniques and Cultural Symbols

*"Traditional Japanese kimono construction uses 43 unique symbols that have remained unchanged for over 400 years, each carrying deep cultural significance."*

## 10.1 Historical and Heritage Technique Markers

Sewing, though universal, has never been a monolithic craft. Across cultures and centuries, distinct traditions have developed their own vocabularies of technique, each accompanied by symbols that act as condensed repositories of knowledge. These historical and heritage markers are not only practical instructions; they are cultural signatures, preserved and transmitted through generations. To decode them is to understand not just how fabric is manipulated, but how entire societies inscribe values, aesthetics, and identities into their clothing. Among the many techniques that rely on specialized symbolic systems, three stand out for their historical depth and enduring relevance: smocking, tambour beading, and goldwork embroidery.

Smocking, which first appeared in medieval Europe, transformed plain cloth into elastic, sculptural surfaces long before elastic fibers existed. The foundation of smocking lies in the smocking plate, a chart marked with grids of geometric dots and lines that guide where fabric should be gathered and stitched. These plates function as symbolic blueprints, each dot representing a gathering point and each line mapping the flow of stitches between them. To the untrained eye, a smocking plate looks like abstract geometry—an arrangement of dots and lines on graph paper—but to the sewist, it is a living code. A diamond grid translates into lattice textures, a honeycomb arrangement into soft elasticity, and a chevron grid into directional ripples. The act of transferring these symbols from plate to fabric requires precision: the dots must be marked consistently, and stitches must follow the prescribed pathways with tension carefully balanced. Too loose, and the design collapses; too tight, and the fabric stiffens unnaturally. Thus, smocking symbols embody both mathematical logic and tactile sensitivity, capturing the interplay of order and flexibility that defines the technique.

While smocking plates map geometry, tambour beading symbols chart rhythm and tension. Tambour embroidery, originating in eighteenth-century France and later flourishing in Indian ateliers, uses a fine hook to chain-stitch beads and sequins onto fabric with speed and precision. Patterns for tambour work are annotated with lines and arrows that indicate beading paths, often marked with dots for bead placement and curves for thread flow. These symbols ensure continuity, preventing breaks in the beaded surface that would weaken the design. Tension indicators are equally important, frequently represented by small marks or annotations specifying the degree of thread slack. Unlike flat embroidery, tambour work requires continuous chains, and any inconsistency in tension disrupts the fluidity of the surface. Symbols that dictate not only where beads should fall but also how tightly the thread should hold them are therefore indispensable. They communicate a choreography of motion: the sweep of the hook, the placement of beads, the give of the thread. For artisans, especially those in couture houses where tambour beading remains a hallmark, these symbols function as a universal script, uniting makers across languages and regions in a shared rhythm of craft.

Goldwork embroidery, perhaps the most symbolically dense of heritage techniques, relies heavily on padding symbols to guide its layered construction. Goldwork does not simply lay metallic threads on fabric; it builds relief through underlayers of felt, string, or parchment, which are then covered with gold thread couched in place. Symbols for this process are typically represented by stacked or shaded diagrams, showing where padding layers must accumulate and in what sequence. A crosshatched area may indicate double padding, while a solid block shows triple padding required for raised elements. Additional notations might signal the direction in which gold threads must be laid, ensuring that light reflects in deliberate patterns. The complexity of these symbols reflects the complexity of the craft itself: goldwork is not flat decoration but sculptural embroidery, demanding planning at multiple levels of depth. Interpreting padding symbols correctly ensures that motifs emerge with dimension and brilliance, whether they adorn ecclesiastical vestments, royal regalia, or ceremonial garments. To misinterpret them is to flatten centuries of tradition into lifeless ornament.

These three symbolic systems—smocking plates, tambour beading paths, and goldwork padding diagrams—demonstrate how sewing symbols are inseparable from cultural heritage. They remind us that clothing has always been more than utility. It is expression, ritual, and identity. Smocking's geometric grids, preserved in European peasant blouses and later in Victorian children's wear, reflect a culture of frugality transformed into elegance. Tambour beading's rhythmic lines, still taught in Parisian couture schools and practiced in Indian workshops, embody cross-cultural exchange and the global movement of fashion. Goldwork's layered diagrams, used in churches and courts for centuries, signify continuity and reverence, transforming garments into vessels of meaning. Each set of symbols is both technical instruction and cultural testimony, bridging generations of makers.

For the modern sewist or designer, encountering these heritage markers is both a challenge and an invitation. The challenge lies in mastering systems that often predate contemporary standards, requiring patience and contextual study. A smocking plate cannot be read like a modern pattern; it must be understood as a grid of potential elasticities. A tambour beading path is not a simple line but a narrative of motion and rhythm. A goldwork padding diagram is not just a map of layers but a vision of light and depth in fabric. To read them correctly requires humility, respect, and a willingness to step into traditions not one's own.

The invitation lies in what these symbols make possible. They offer access to techniques that expand the vocabulary of modern fashion, allowing designers to enrich contemporary garments with echoes of the past. A dress incorporating smocked panels brings elasticity without synthetic fibers. A gown adorned with tambour beading achieves a shimmer no machine can replicate. A stole embroidered with goldwork carries gravitas that transcends trend. Symbols preserve these possibilities, ensuring that they are not lost to time but remain available to those willing to learn their language.

The persistence of these symbols across centuries also testifies to their effectiveness. While technology has transformed many aspects of sewing notation, smocking plates still rely on grids, tambour paths still use dots and lines, and goldwork padding diagrams still layer shading and crosshatching. Their longevity suggests that the best symbols are not arbitrary but deeply intuitive, capturing the essence of a technique in forms that transcend language and culture. They are proof that visual grammar, once refined, can endure even as materials and contexts change.

Errors in interpreting heritage symbols can be especially telling. A smocking design stitched without proper attention to dot spacing produces uneven elasticity, betraying inexperience. A tambour line beaded with incorrect tension loses its rhythm, beads slipping or puckering fabric. A goldwork motif padded incorrectly appears flat, dull, and lifeless, its brilliance dimmed before the gold is even applied. These mistakes illustrate why symbols matter: they are not decorative additions but essential tools for maintaining integrity in complex traditions.

Ultimately, historical and heritage technique markers remind us that sewing symbols are more than just technical aids. They are cultural artifacts, repositories of values and aesthetics transmitted across generations. Each dot, line, and shaded zone is part of a lineage, carrying with it the weight of history and the continuity of craft. To study them is to engage not only with fabric but with the cultures that shaped them, to recognize that symbols can encode identity as much as instruction.

## 10.2 Cultural and Regional Specialties

Sewing symbols do not exist only in the realm of standardized manuals or couture ateliers; they also carry the weight of cultural tradition. Around the world, regional garment systems have developed their own unique forms of notation, many of which reflect not just technical demands but also cultural values and social identities. These symbols often emerged to solve specific problems—how to manage vast quantities of cloth, how to maintain uniformity in ceremonial dress, or how to preserve decorative placement within cultural motifs. In decoding them, one uncovers both the logic of construction and the symbolic meaning of garments themselves.

The sari, perhaps one of the most iconic garments of South Asia, exemplifies this fusion of practicality and tradition. Unlike cut-and-sewn garments, a sari is a single length of fabric that relies entirely on folding, pleating, and draping. Symbols used in sari construction and draping are therefore not about cutting lines but about placement and sequence. Draping markers, often represented in tailoring diagrams as arrows, dots, or lines along the selvedge, show where pleats should begin, where the pallu (the decorative end) must be placed over the shoulder, and how the fabric should be anchored at the waist. Regional variations add further symbolic layers. In Bengal, markers emphasize broader front pleats, while in Maharashtra, symbols indicate the creation of trouser-like folds at the legs. In Tamil Nadu, the pallu's wrap-around is guided by marks that dictate its length and layering. Each variation relies on symbolic shorthand that ensures the cultural integrity of the drape is maintained. To misinterpret these markers is to risk losing not only functionality but also the cultural identity encoded in the sari's presentation.

In Scotland, the kilt carries its own precise symbolic system, rooted in military tradition. Kilts are constructed from tartan wool, where pleating must align with the plaid's vertical and horizontal lines. Symbols here often take the form of mathematical notations paired with pleat markers. A line across the tartan may be annotated to show "sett width," the repeating unit of the plaid, while pleating calculations are indicated by arrows and ratios that reveal how many threads should be taken into each pleat. In military kilts, additional symbols codify the number of pleats per soldier, ensuring that uniforms across regiments remain consistent. These specifications are not arbitrary; they maintain visual harmony during parades and battles, where the uniformity of pleats is as much about discipline as it is about appearance. Reading kilt pleating symbols is therefore an act of interpreting military order as much as textile logic. A pleat slightly misaligned disrupts not only the flow of fabric but the symbolic unity of an entire regiment.

Embroidery traditions around the world provide further examples of culturally rich symbolic systems. In Eastern Europe, embroidery placement symbols are used to map motifs on blouses, aprons, and headscarves. These marks often appear as grids of dots and lines superimposed over garment outlines, indicating where specific motifs—floral, geometric, or symbolic—should be stitched. In Central Asia, placement symbols guide the layout of suzani embroideries, ensuring that motifs radiate symmetrically across wall hangings or ceremonial textiles. In Mexico, huipil embroidery relies on markers that divide garments into symbolic quadrants, each representing aspects of the cosmos or community identity. These placement diagrams are not only practical guides for artisans but also carriers of intangible heritage. They ensure that motifs retain their intended meaning across generations, preserving cultural knowledge through visual shorthand.

Together, sari draping markers, kilt pleating calculations, and embroidery placement symbols highlight how sewing notation adapts to cultural needs. They remind us that symbols are not just technical marks but cultural artifacts. To read them correctly is to honor the traditions they encode, to recognize that each arrow, dot, or ratio embodies not only construction but also heritage. They reveal that the global lexicon of sewing is far from uniform; it is a mosaic of specialized grammars, each shaped by the histories and values of the communities that created them.

## 10.3 Adaptive and Therapeutic Garment Symbols

As sewing symbols preserve cultural traditions, they also expand into new territories of human need, particularly in adaptive and therapeutic clothing. Here, the symbolic language of sewing takes on a humanitarian role, guiding the construction of garments that prioritize accessibility, comfort, and medical accommodation. These symbols do not emerge from centuries of tradition but from urgent contemporary concerns: how to design clothing for those with limited mobility, sensory sensitivities, or medical devices. Their presence on patterns reflects the growing recognition that clothing must serve diverse bodies, not just idealized or average forms.

Accessibility modification points are among the most significant symbols in adaptive garment design. These markers, often represented by specialized arrows or segmented lines, indicate areas where closures must be altered for easier dressing. For example, a traditional back zipper may be replaced with a side-opening system, marked by a distinct accessibility symbol. Other notations may show where hook-and-loop fasteners replace buttons, or where magnets are inserted to assist individuals with limited dexterity. These symbols ensure that garments can be constructed to facilitate independence, reducing the physical strain of dressing. For sewists interpreting these marks, the challenge is not only technical but empathetic: to understand that the placement of a closure may determine whether a garment empowers or frustrates its wearer.

Sensory-friendly seam indicators represent another important development. For individuals with autism or heightened tactile sensitivity, conventional seams may cause discomfort, irritation, or distraction. Symbols for sensory seams often appear as shaded or dashed overlays along seam allowances, accompanied by annotations specifying flat construction, soft binding, or outward-facing allowances. These marks communicate that the seam must be engineered to minimize tactile disruption, whether by turning seams outward, enclosing them in soft tape, or using seamless bonding technology. The symbols transform an abstract concern—comfort for sensitive skin—into concrete construction guidance, allowing sewists to produce garments that are not only wearable but truly supportive.

Medical device accommodation symbols extend this adaptive vocabulary further. In garments designed for individuals with insulin pumps, feeding tubes, or cardiac monitors, access panels and reinforcement zones are critical. These symbols typically appear as rectangles, circles, or flaps annotated on the garment diagram, indicating precisely where openings must be inserted. Accompanying arrows may show how panels open, whether with zippers, snaps, or concealed Velcro. Reinforcement symbols may also appear, guiding the addition of stabilizing layers to prevent fabric from tearing under repeated use. These notations ensure that garments integrate with medical devices seamlessly, avoiding the need for constant adjustments or improvisations by the wearer. In effect, they transform garments into therapeutic tools, designed to support health as much as style.

The rise of adaptive and therapeutic garment symbols illustrates the inclusivity of modern sewing notation. Where traditional symbols focused on aesthetic precision or cultural continuity, these marks address dignity, accessibility, and care. They expand the symbolic lexicon to include human diversity in its fullest sense, acknowledging that clothing must adapt to bodies, not the other way around.

For sewists, learning these symbols is an act of both technical mastery and ethical engagement. To interpret accessibility points is to ensure that someone with limited mobility can dress independently. To follow sensory seam markers is to create comfort for someone overwhelmed by touch. To place medical device panels correctly is to give ease and confidence to someone managing chronic illness. These symbols remind us that sewing is not merely about fashion but about humanity, and that every mark carries the potential to improve lives.

# Conclusion

Every stitch begins as an idea, but every idea needs a guide to reach its final form. Sewing symbols, those small and often overlooked marks scattered across patterns, are far more than instructional shorthand. They are the invisible architecture of the making process, the silent partners that ensure precision, continuity, and connection. Over the course of this book, we have walked through their histories, examined their functions, and traced their evolution from medieval guild ciphers to digital animation icons. What becomes clear is that these marks are not marginal details. They are the essence of communication in sewing, the shared grammar that makes fabric transformation possible across cultures, centuries, and technologies.

To understand sewing symbols is to appreciate their dual role as both practical tools and cultural artifacts. On one hand, they make construction possible, guiding where to cut, fold, and stitch. On the other, they preserve the knowledge of generations, codifying methods that might otherwise vanish with the passing of oral traditions. When you trace a dart symbol, you are not just shaping fabric—you are enacting a practice refined through centuries of tailoring. When you align notches, you are following the same logic that allowed industrial factories to produce garments with astonishing consistency. When you interpret a pleat or gather mark, you are part of a lineage that includes European smockers, Japanese kimono makers, and countless unnamed artisans who contributed to the visual grammar we now take for granted.

Symbols are efficient because they condense complex instructions into a single visual cue. But they are also democratic, allowing knowledge to move beyond words. A person who does not read a given written language can still follow a line of arrows, dots, or shading, and produce a garment identical to one made continents away. This universality makes sewing symbols not only a language but also a community. They are what allow a sewist in Nairobi to follow a pattern drafted in Paris, or a hobbyist in Buenos Aires to assemble a design from Seoul. In every case, the marks transcend linguistic barriers, providing clarity where words might fail.

The future of sewing symbols is as fascinating as their past. In the digital age, they have moved beyond the static page. Parametric systems adjust automatically to body size, layer-based symbols organize complexity in CAD software, and animation icons demonstrate construction sequences in motion. Smart textiles demand new markers for conductive pathways and sensor placements, while laser cutting and 3D printing introduce notations that machines interpret directly. Yet despite these innovations, the core principles remain unchanged. Whether drawn by hand on parchment, printed in a factory pattern, or generated by software, the purpose of the symbol is the same: to guide the transformation of flat fabric into structured, wearable form.

There is a paradox here that gives sewing symbols their enduring power. They are at once humble and monumental. On the page, they are no more than lines, dots, arrows, and grids—marks a child might scribble without meaning. But in context, they are the distillation of centuries of ingenuity. Each symbol carries with it not only technical instruction but also trust: trust that the maker can follow it, that the fabric will respond as expected, and that the garment will emerge as intended. Symbols act as a bridge between designer and sewist, between idea and execution, between tradition and innovation.

For the modern maker, fluency in this language is a form of empowerment. It eliminates hesitation, turning confusion into clarity. It allows a pattern to be read not as an intimidating map of alien marks but as a story waiting to be enacted. Grainlines cease to be abstract arrows and become promises of stability. Dart symbols transform from simple triangles into sculptural cues for shaping. Pleat markers evolve from parallel lines into orchestrated rhythms of volume. Each symbol is not a demand but an invitation: follow me, and the garment will come alive.

Yet symbols do more than guarantee precision; they open the door to creativity. Once the language is mastered, it becomes flexible. A sewist who understands dart rotation symbols can alter silhouettes with confidence, turning shaping into design. One who grasps pleat depth notation can play with proportion, exaggerating or softening fullness. A reader fluent in finishing symbols can choose between efficiency and refinement, deciding when to serge, when to bind, when to turn and stitch. Mastery frees the maker from dependence, allowing patterns to become frameworks for innovation rather than strict rules. In this way, symbols nurture independence, enabling sewists to move from following to inventing.

The cultural dimension of sewing symbols cannot be overlooked. They are more than technical tools; they are repositories of heritage. Smocking grids preserve the ingenuity of medieval Europe. Kilt pleating markers encode Scottish military precision. Sari draping arrows maintain the integrity of Indian regional styles. Goldwork padding diagrams protect traditions of ceremonial embroidery. Adaptive garment symbols reflect contemporary values of inclusivity, ensuring that clothing can accommodate diverse bodies and needs. Every system of notation is also a record of the society that created it, a silent archive in marks and lines. By learning to read them, one not only gains technical skill but also participates in a cultural dialogue that spans continents and centuries.

Errors remind us why symbols matter. A dart sewn to the wrong apex distorts an entire bodice. A zipper misaligned with its placement marks renders a garment awkward. A pleat folded in the wrong direction changes the flow of a skirt. A missed notch in industrial production can waste thousands of garments. Symbols are safeguards, ensuring that intention becomes execution, that mistakes are minimized, and that garments emerge consistent and functional. They do not eliminate human error, but they provide guardrails that protect against it, embedding discipline into the making process.

Looking ahead, sewing symbols will continue to evolve alongside technology, but their essence will remain constant. As augmented reality overlays project fold lines directly onto fabric, as AI-assisted systems recommend seam finishes based on fabric choice, as 3D printers merge with textiles, the marks will adapt. They will gain new layers of meaning and new modes of interaction, but they will still serve the same fundamental role: to communicate clearly, efficiently, and universally. They will still be the grammar of making, the silent instructions that transform intention into form.

For readers of this book, the goal is not simply to memorize marks but to cultivate fluency. To become fluent in sewing symbols is to gain the ability to interpret, adapt, and innovate. It is to join a global community of makers who share not just fabric and thread but also a language. It is to step into a lineage of knowledge that stretches back to guild halls, through factory floors, into couture ateliers, and now across digital platforms. It is to recognize that in every dot, arrow, or line lies a story: of craft, of culture, of creativity.

The conclusion, then, is simple yet profound. Sewing symbols are more than technical notation. They are the universal language of making, the visual grammar that connects individuals across borders and generations. They enable garments to be more than fabric stitched together; they allow clothing to embody precision, meaning, and beauty. To study them is to honor the past, embrace the present, and prepare for the future of craft. They remind us that while fabrics change, while technologies advance, while fashions shift, the need for clear communication between designer and maker remains constant. Symbols are that communication, condensed into lines and marks that continue to guide us.

In your hands now is not just a dictionary of sewing symbols but a key to a wider world. With it, you can approach any pattern, from the simplest tote bag to the most complex couture gown, with confidence. You can interpret, you can adapt, and you can create. You are part of a community that shares this language, one that stretches far beyond your own sewing table. And as you move forward, every arrow, dot, and line you decode will remind you of this truth: sewing is not just craft, not just industry, not just tradition. It is a universal dialogue, carried forward in symbols that speak without words, a conversation in stitches that continues to connect makers worldwide.

www.ingramcontent.com/pod-product-compliance
Lightning Source LLC
Chambersburg PA
CBHW071137090426
42736CB00012B/2142